More sketches from the English Teaching Theatre

FURTHER OFF-STAGE!

DOUG CASE
& KEN WILSON

STUDENTS' BOOK

Photographs by Richard Gibb and Paddy Eckersley

HEINEMANN EDUCATIONAL BOOKS LONDON

Heinemann Educational Books Ltd

22 Bedford Square, London WC1B 3HH
LONDON EDINBURGH MELBOURNE AUCKLAND
HONG KONG SINGAPORE KUALA LUMPUR NEW DELHI
IBADAN NAIROBI JOHANNESBURG
PORTSMOUTH (NH) KINGSTON PORT OF SPAIN

ISBN 0 435 28000 7
(Teachers' Book ISBN 0 435 28001 5)
(Audio Cassette ISBN 0 435 28002 3)
(VHS Video Cassette ISBN 0 435 28003 1)
(Betamax Video Cassette ISBN 0 435 28004 X)
© Doug Case and Ken Wilson 1984
First Published 1984
Reprinted 1986

Text set in 10/13 Oracle II by Georgia Origination, Liverpool
Printed and bound in Great Britain by Butler & Tanner Ltd
Frome and London

The authors and publishers would like to thank the
following for permission to reproduce their material
and for providing illustrations:

TV Times and the National Dairy Council – **p. 10**;
What's On and Where to Go in London, Chez Solange
Restaurant Francais, Ristorante Bacco '70, Choy's
Chinese Restaurant, Sakura Japanese Restaurant,
Vogue Indian Restaurant, Don Pepe Spanish
Restaurant – **pp. 24** and **25**; Camera Press and Mary
Evans Picture Library – **p. 33**; HMSO – **pp. 41** and **56**;
British Telecom – **p. 42**; London Transport Executive –
pp. 48 and **49**; Barnaby's Picture Library – **pp. 48** and
49; Malvin van Gelderen **p. 49**; British Railways Board
– **pp. 55** and **71**; BBC, ITV, Rolls Royce Motors,
QANTAS Airways Ltd, British Airways, Transworld
Airlines, Ministry of Defence – **p. 56**; République
Populaire de Pologne; General Directorate of Posts,
Norway; Postal Ministry, People's Republic of China;
Bundesrepublik Deutschland and Mr Erik Nitsche;
Postmaster General, Athens; Tokyo Central Post
Office; PTT Bern; Philatelia Hungarica; The Post
Office, London – **p. 79**.

Acknowledgements

As in our previous book of ETT sketches, *Off-stage!*, we
would like to express our thanks to many people:

— to John Haycraft, for having the original idea for
  the ETT, and for constant support and
  encouragement ever since;
— to Jeremy Harrison and Piers Plowright, who first
  gave the ETT a style and identity;
— to all the members of the ETT, past and present,
  particularly to those who performed the sketches
  in this book with us during the 1979–83 tours:
  Andy Whitfield, Brian Bowles, Bridget Lynch-
  Blosse, Cliff Burnett, Coralyn Sheldon, David
  Lochner, Ginny Clee, Hazel Imbert, Hilary Waters,
  Hugh Trethowan, Jenny Joenn, John Colclough,
  Judy Garton-Sprenger, Kieran Fogarty, Kit Jackson,
  Koni McCurdy, Lawrence Fitzgerald, Mac
  Andrews, Nick Jones, Richard Piper, Roy Garner,
  Sheelagh Gilbey, Steve Wallace, Sue Chiverton,
  Tim Barron, Terry Tomscha and William
  Gaminara;
— to all the organizations who have helped us with
  our tours, particularly International House, the
  British Council, BBC English by Radio & TV, the
  British Tourist Authority, British Airways and British
  Caledonian Airways;
— and most of all, to all the teachers and students
  who have been our audiences, organizers and
  hosts, for their help, kindness, hospitality and
  enthusiasm.

Dedication

This book is dedicated to our friend, Lawrence
Fitzgerald, who died in 1981. Lawrence had been a
member of the ETT since 1977, and made us laugh
more often than almost anyone we've known.

Doug Case
Ken Wilson
May 1983

Contents

Introduction

This is the second book of sketches taken from shows performed by the English Teaching Theatre. (The first was *Off-stage!*, which appeared in 1979, and included sketches from the 1974–78 shows.) The sketches in this book are taken from shows performed on tours between 1979 and 1983. We hope you will enjoy listening to them, reading them and re-enacting them yourselves.

The ETT is a unique kind of theatre. It began in 1969 at International House, London, when the director, John Haycraft, said to one of his teachers, Jeremy Harrison: 'Why don't we have a theatre specially for students of English?'

For several years, there were summer seasons in London, and since 1974 the ETT has been a permanent theatre-group. Its members are teachers, actors and musicians, who spend eight months of each year on tour, performing in schools, teacher-training colleges, universities and theatres all over the world. Every year, more than 250 performances are given, and the show is seen on stage by more than 75,000 people – and on TV by many more.

Between 1973 and 1983, the ETT performed in these countries: Argentina, Austria, Belgium, Brazil, Colombia, Cyprus, Denmark, Ecuador, Egypt, France, Germany, Greece, Holland, Iceland, Israel, Italy, Japan, Mexico, Norway, Peru, Portugal, Spain, Sweden, Switzerland, Turkey, Venezuela and Yugoslavia.

The sketches in this book are accompanied by:

- Questions
- Puzzles
- Reading and writing exercises

and — very importantly:

- 'Communicating' and
- 'In your own words' exercises.

These are important because (as John Haycraft said when talking about the beginnings of the ETT)

'English is not just words, structures and idioms; it is a lively, dramatic and versatile means of communication'.

We hope you enjoy the sketches in *Further Off-Stage!* – and that we may see you 'on stage' with the ETT one day.

Photographs

The photographs in this book show the following performers:

Tea break   Brian, Coralyn, David, Koni, Roy
The King of Boonland   Hugh, Kieran
The restaurant   Hazel, Hugh, John, Koni
The passport office   Hazel, Ken
Fire practice   Hazel, Ken, Nick, Sue
The bus stop   Hazel, Hugh, Kieran, Koni
A ticket to Birmingham   Hugh, John
Gerry Thatcher's party   Coralyn, Hugh, Ken, Kieran
The lost property office   Hazel, Ken
Mr Universe   Brian, Kieran, Koni

1 Tea break

Scene A rehearsal room in a theatre

Characters Five actors, taking a tea break:
Tom, Jerry, Jane, Martin, Sara

Jerry All right. That's enough. It's time for a cup of tea.
Tom Oh, good. A cup of tea. I can't wait.

Jerry, Jane, Martin and Sara sit down. There is no chair for Tom.

Jane OK, Tom, make the tea.
Tom Me?
Sara Yes, make the tea.
Tom Make the tea? Me?
Jane Why not?
Tom All right. What do I have to do? I mean, how do you make tea?
Jerry Huh! He doesn't know how to make tea!
Tom OK, Jerry. How *do* you make tea?
Jerry Er . . . I don't know.

5

The others laugh.

II	Martin	Listen, Tom — it's easy. Put some water in the kettle.
	Sara	Put the kettle on the stove.
	Jane	Light a match.
	Martin	Turn on the gas.
	Sara	And light the gas.
	Jane	Then put some tea in the teapot —
	Tom	It sounds a bit complicated.
	Jane	Oh, come on! It's easy!
	Martin	Listen, Tom. You don't have to make the tea.
	Tom	Oh, good.
	Martin	You can get some from the café.
	Tom	Oh. OK. See you later.

Tom goes towards the door.

III	Jerry	Wait a minute!
	Tom	What?
	Jane	You don't know what we want yet.
	Tom	Oh, yes. Sorry. What do you all want? Sara?
	Sara	I'd like a cup of tea — with no milk and no sugar.
	Tom	One tea — no milk, no sugar. Jane?
	Jane	I'd like a cup of tea — with lots of milk and no sugar.
	Tom	Lots of milk — no tea. Right.
	Jane	No *sugar*!
	Tom	No sugar. Right. Jerry?
	Jerry	I'd like a lemon tea and a big cream cake.
	Tom	A lemon cake and a cream tea.
	Jerry	Careful!
	Tom	What do *you* want, Martin?
	Martin	A whisky and soda.
	Tom	With milk and sugar?
	Martin	Of course.

IV ***Tom wants to check the orders.***

	Tom	OK. Let me get this right. Sara, you want a cup of tea, with no milk and no sugar.
	Sara	Yes. Er . . . No. On second thoughts, I think I'd prefer *coffee*.
	Tom	Coffee.
	Sara	Yes, a cup of coffee — with milk and sugar.
	Tom	Right. So — it's one *coffee* with milk and sugar, and one *tea* with milk and sugar.
	Jane	*No* sugar.
	Tom	No sugar. Right. Jerry, you want a lemon tea and a big cream cake.
	Jerry	*In* the tea.
	Tom	*In* the tea.
	Jerry	That's right.

Tom	And Martin — you want a whisky and soda.
Martin	With milk and sugar.
Tom	With milk and sugar. Right. OK. See you in a minute.

V   ***Tom leaves. Very soon, he comes back.***

Tom	Right. Here you are. One coffee and soda, one whisky and cream, one lemon and milk, and one big sugar cake. All right?
Jane	Martin?
Martin	Yes?
Jane	Go and make some tea.

About the sketch

Say if these sentences are *true* or *false*.

I   **1**   Tom knows how to make tea.
     2   Jerry knows how to make tea.
II **3**   To make tea, you first put some water in a teapot.
     4   You put the teapot on the stove.
     5   The café does not have a take-away service.
     6   The café is near the theatre.
III **7**   Jerry likes cream cakes.
     8   Martin never drinks alcohol.
IV **9**   Sara never drinks coffee.
V **10** Tom asks 'All right?' The answer to this question is 'Yes, fine'.

Communicating

1 Asking and explaining how to do something

Look at these lines from the sketch:

> How do you make tea?
> It's easy. Put some water in the kettle.
> Put the kettle on the stove.
> Light a match. (. . .)

A   In pairs, ask and explain how to do these things:
– make coffee
– make a tomato sandwich
– get to the nearest railway station.

B   A visitor to your country asks you these questions:
– How do you make a telephone call from a public telephone?
– How do you get a taxi?
Can you answer?

2 Saying what you'd like to drink

Look at these lines from the sketch:

ASKING		ANSWERING	
Tom	What do you all want? Sara?	**Sara**	I'd like a cup of tea.
	Jane?	**Jane**	I'd like a cup of tea.
	Right. Jerry?	**Jerry**	I'd like a lemon tea.
	What do you want, Martin?	**Martin**	A whisky and soda.
MORE POLITELY		MORE POLITELY	
What would you all like? What would *you* like, Martin?		A whisky and soda, please.	

Make conversations in groups of five. One person asks the questions. The others say what they would like to drink. The first person must remember the orders. Take turns as the person asking the questions.

3 Changing your mind

Look at these lines from the sketch:

> **Tom**   Sara, you want a cup of tea, with no milk and no sugar.
> **Sara**   Yes. Er . . . No. On second thoughts, I think I'd prefer *coffee*.

If you change your mind, you can also say:

> Can I change my mind?
> Sorry. I've changed my mind.   I think I'd prefer . . .

Do Exercise 2 again. This time, you can change your mind if you like.

Question time

Here are eight answers to questions about the sketch:

1   Jerry.
2   Martin.
3   Tom and Jerry.
4   Martin, Sara and Jane.
5   Yes, it is.
6   No, he doesn't.
7   Yes, it has.
8   Yes, she does.

Put them after the right questions.

A Who knows how to make tea?
B Who doesn't know how to make tea?
C Who likes cream cakes?
D Who likes whisky and soda with milk and sugar?
E Has the café got a take-away service?
F Is the café near the theatre?
G Does Sara know how to make tea?
H Does Tom know how to make tea?

Reading: A notice in a café

THE CORNER CAFÉ

	HAVE HERE	TAKE AWAY
TEA WITH MILK	20p	17p
LEMON TEA	22p	18p
BLACK COFFEE	28p	23p
WHITE COFFEE	25p	21p
LEMONADE	25p	21p
COCA-COLA	30p	24p
ORANGE JUICE	25p	21p
TOMATO SANDWICH	50p	45p
CHEESE SANDWICH	40p	35p
CHEESE AND TOM. SANDWICH	45p	40p
HAM SANDWICH	50p	45p
EGG SANDWICH	40p	35p
CHICKEN SANDWICH	55p	50p
CREAM CAKE	25p	21p

1 You go to the café with this take-away order:
Two white coffees, one coca-cola, one lemon tea, one egg sandwich, two cheese sandwiches and one cream cake.
How much is it?

2 How much is the same order, if you and your friends stay in the café?

Writing: Notes and instructions

1 These are Tom's notes. What do his abbreviations mean?

S: tea ~~no~~ m.   coffee
        no s.   (m+s)
Ja: tea, lots of m.
        no s.
Je: lemon tea, big c. cake
M: w+s. (+m.+s.)

Do this exercise in groups of five:
Four people give their orders and the fifth person notes them down on a piece of paper.
The fifth person then reads out the orders, to check them. The others can change their minds, if they like. If they change their minds, the fifth person changes the notes, and finally reads them out to check again.

2 Complete this list of instructions. Look at the pictures and Section **II** of the sketch, if necessary.

HOW TO MAKE TEA
1 Put some . . . . in the . . . .
2 Put the . . . . on the . . . .
3 Light a . . . .
4 Turn on the . . . .
5 . . . . the gas.
6 Put some tea in the . . . .
7 When the . . . . boils, pour it into the . . . .
8 Leave the tea for . . . .
9 Pour the . . . . into the . . . .
10 Add . . . . and . . . . if you like.

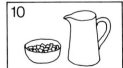

In your own words

Re-enact the sketch in your own words, without reading from the text. Do it in short sections. These words will remind you.

I	II	III	IV	V
a cup of tea make the tea How?	the kettle the gas the teapot the café	What do you all want?	Let me get this right. on second thoughts See you...	Here you are. make some tea

Word puzzle

Put the correct words in the horizontal boxes. All the words are in the sketch.

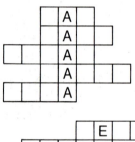

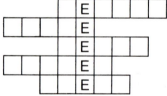

Extra!

A recipe from Wales

Here is a recipe for a very simple Welsh dish.

Welsh Rarebit

Enough for 2

(225g) mature Cheddar cheese
(15g) butter
dash of Worcestershire sauce
1 teaspoon (5ml) mustard powder
1 tablespoon (15ml) flour
4 tablespoons (60ml) milk
salt and pepper
4 large slices bread
Grate the cheese and melt in a saucepan. Stir in all the other ingredients except the bread. Toast the bread, spread with mixture and grill. Serve immediately.

It's just right for a quick snack — have a cup of tea with it!

2 The King of Boonland

Scene   In front of Buckingham Palace

Characters   A guard
A sergeant
The King of Boonland

The guard and the sergeant march to the sentry-box.

Sergeant   Quick march! Left, right, left, right, left, right, left, right! Halt! . . . Right turn!

Sergeant   Bradshaw!
Guard   Sir!
Sergeant   You are guarding Buckingham Palace.
Guard   Yes, sir!
Sergeant   Don't forget!
Guard   No, sir!

The sergeant leaves. The guard stands silently. The King of Boonland comes up to the guard.

11

II	**King**	Good morning . . . Hallo? . . . Nice day, isn't it? . . . Do you speak English? . . . Sprechen Sie espanol? . . . I think he's deaf. Oh, well . . .

The King starts to go into the Palace.

Guard	Oi!
King	Oh! He can talk!
Guard	Where are you going?
King	I'm going into Buckingham Palace.
Guard	Stand there!
King	I don't want to stand there. I want to go in there.
Guard	Stand there!!
King	Oh, all right.
Guard	Who do you think you are?
King	I'm Fred, King of Boonland.
Guard	Well, listen to me, Fred King —
King	No, no, my name isn't Fred King. I am King Fred.
Guard	Are you trying to tell me that *you* are a real king?
King	Yes. I am the King of Boonland.
Guard	Boonland?
King	Yes.
Guard	And where exactly is Boonland?
King	Huh! You don't know where Boonland is?
Guard	No.
King	Oh. OK, look at my map . . .

The King finds his map.

	. . . yes, here we are. Now, this is a map of the world.
Guard	Yes.
King	And Boonland is *here*.
Guard	*That* is the Atlantic Ocean.
King	Yes — and Boonland is in the middle.
Guard	What? In the middle of the Atlantic?
King	Yes.

III	**Guard**	I don't believe you.
	King	Eh?
	Guard	I think you are trying to get into Buckingham Palace.
	King	That's right. I am.
	Guard	Well, you can't.
	King	Yes, I can. Wait a minute — I can prove I'm the King of Boonland. Look!
	Guard	It's a five-pound note.
	King	No, it's not five *pounds*.
	Guard	Isn't it?
	King	No, it's five *boonos*.
	Guard	Five *boonos*?

King   Yes.

The guard looks at the note.

Guard   Oh, yes! Five boonos. So this is the money you use in Boonland.

King   Yes, it is.

Guard   How many boonos are there in a pound?

King   Half a million.

Guard   Half a million?!

King   Yes, and there are one hundred *boonitos* in a boono.

Guard   Now, listen to me —

King   Ah! I can prove I'm the King of Boonland. There's a picture of me on the one-boonito coin. Um . . . Have you got change for ten boonitos?

Guard   No, I haven't!

King   Oh. It's all right. Look — one boonito coin, with a picture of me on it.

Guard   *That* is a picture of a monkey.

King   What? Oh, sorry. The other side.

Guard   Oh, yes. A picture of you.

The King nods.

IV   **Guard**   Tell me — why do you want to go into the Palace?

King   I am here to bring the Queen the good wishes of the people of Boonland.

Guard   The good wishes of the people of Boonland?

King	Yes.
Guard	How many people are there in Boonland?
King	Well, there's *me*, and *my mother*, and —
Guard	No, no! *All together!* What's the *population* of Boonland?
King	Ah — well, there are the people in the capital —
Guard	In the capital?
King	Yes, Boonland City. And there are the people who live in the mountains — we call them 'the mountain people'.
Guard	Very clever.
King	And there are the people who live in the lake.
Guard	In the lake?!
King	Yes.
Guard	What do you call them?
King	Stupid.

They laugh.

Guard	So, there are the people in the capital —
King	Boonland City.
Guard	— and the people who live in the mountains —
King	The mountain people.
Guard	— and the people who live in the lake.
King	The idiots.
Guard	How many is that all together?
King	Fourteen.
Guard	Fourteen?!

V

King	Yes. And we want to give the Queen a special Boonese present.
Guard	A special present from Boonland?
King	Yes — here it is!

The King takes a banana from his bag.

Guard	But that's a banana.
King	I know.
Guard	What's so special about a banana?
King	It isn't an ordinary banana.
Guard	Isn't it?
King	No. Put it in your ear.
Guard	What?!
King	Put the banana in your ear.
Guard	Why?
King	Just put the banana in your ear.
Guard	All right.

The guard puts the banana in his ear

King	Can you hear anything?
Guard	Oh, yes!

King	What does it sound like?
Guard	It sounds like an elephant with toothache.
King	What?! *That* is the National Song of Boonland. (*He sings:*) Oh, Boonland! */!*&*@::!*/!*
Guard	Oi!
King	It's all right — I'm speaking Boonese. */!* is a word in Boonese.
Guard	And what exactly does */!* mean?
King	It means 'land of sunshine and bananas'.

The King sneezes.

Guard	What does *that* mean?
King	It means I've got a bad cold. Now give me the banana, because I don't want to be late for tea with the Queen.
Guard	Oh, right, sir. Here you are, sir.

The guard gives back the banana.

King	Thank you very much. Oh, this is for you.
Guard	What is it?
King	Half a million boonos.
Guard	Half a million boonos?!
King	Yes. Go and buy yourself a cup of tea.

About the sketch

Choose the right words.

I 1 Bradshaw is *a guard/a sergeant*.
II 2 He and the King are *inside/outside* the Palace.
   3 Boonland is in the middle of *the Pacific/the Atlantic*.
III 4 The currency of Boonland is *the pound/the boono*.
   5 The one-boonito coin *has/has not* got a picture of the King on it.
   6 There are a hundred boonitos in a *pound/a boono*.
IV 7 The capital of Boonland is *Boonland City/Boonland Town*.
   8 Boonland has a *large/small* population.
V 9 The Boonese language *sounds/does not sound* like English.
   10 Boonland is probably a *hot/cold* country.

Communicating

1 Telling someone about your country

Look at these lines from the sketch:

> Boonland is in the middle of the Atlantic Ocean.
> There are one hundred boonitos in a boono.
> (The capital is) Boonland City.
> */!* is a word in Boonese.

Say these things about *your* country:

> I come from . . .
> It's { near . . .
>   { to the N/S/E/W of . . .
>   { an island in the . . .
> The capital is . . .
> The population is about . . .
> The currency is . . .
> We speak . . .

2 Finding out about someone's country

Look at these lines from the sketch:

> Where exactly is Boonland?
> How many boonos are there in a pound?
> { How many people are there in Boonland? }
> { What is the population of Boonland?   }

Practise in pairs. One person wants to find out about the other person's country.

Find out about these things . . .	by using these questions . . .
Location	Where (exactly) is . . . ?
Capital City	What is the capital (city)?
Population	{ What is the population?
	{ How many people are there in . . . ?
Currency	What is the currency of . . . ?
Language	What language do you speak?

Begin: Where do you come from?

3 Correcting someone politely

Look at the information in this table:

	NEW ZEALAND	AUSTRALIA	CANADA	BOONLAND
LOCATION	in the SE Pacific	between the Indian Ocean and the Pacific	to the north of the USA	in the middle of the Atlantic
CAPITAL	Wellington	Canberra	Ottawa	Boonland City
POP.	3m	14m	23m	14
CURRENCY	the New Zealand dollar	the Australian dollar	the Canadian dollar	the boono
LANGUAGE	English	English	English and French	Boonese

Make dialogues like this:

> A The capital of Canada is Canberra.
> B { Are you sure?
>   { No, I don't think that's right.
> A Oh, no. Sorry. *Ottawa*.

> A There are 13 million people in New Zealand.
> B { Are you sure?
>   { No, I don't think that's right.
> A Oh, no. Sorry. *Three* million.

Question time

Here are ten answers. (Five are about Boonland, five are about other countries). What are the questions?

1 ....? Fourteen.
2 ....? One hundred.
3 ....? Boonland City.
4 ....? Half a million.
5 ....? In the middle of the Atlantic.
6 ....? The peseta.
7 ....? Lisbon.
8 ....? Between France and the Netherlands.
9 ....? To the south of Colombia, and to the north of Peru.
10 ....? The baht.

Reading:
An encyclopaedia entry

Read this description of Boonland from the 'World Encyclopaedia', and find the mistakes in it.

> BOONLAND   A small island in the middle of the Pacific Ocean. A republic. The head of state is Fred King, and he never leaves the island.
> There is a large population, mainly in the capital, Boonsville. The country has a lot of mountains, but no lakes.
> The language of Boonland is Spanish, and the unit of currency is the boono (about 100 to the pound sterling). There are ten boonitos in a boono. There is a picture of an elephant on the one-boonito coin.

Writing:
A description of your country

Complete this form for your country:

NAME OF COUNTRY :	....
LOCATION :	....
HEAD OF STATE :	....
POPULATION :	....
CAPITAL CITY :	....
LANGUAGE :	....
UNIT OF CURRENCY :	....

Use your notes to write a description of your country for the 'World Encyclopaedia'.

In your own words

Re-enact the sketch in your own words, without reading from the text. Do it in short sections. These words will remind you.

I	II	III	IV	V
Left, right! Buckingham Palace	Stand there! Who? Where? the Atlantic Ocean	5 boonos half a million picture of me a monkey	good wishes How many? city mountains lake	present banana Can you hear? National Song

Word puzzle

The answers to this puzzle are all cities, countries, provinces or rivers.

```
B _ _ _ _ _ _
O _ _ _ _ _
O _ _
N _ _ _ _ _ _ _ _
L _ _ / _ _ _ _ _
A _ _ _ _ _ _ _
N _ _ _
D _ _ _ _ _
```

A Scandinavian capital
A city in the west of England
A country between Germany and Belgium
A Canadian province   An island continent
The capital of the Irish Republic
The longest river in the world
A large city in California

Extra!

Nationalities

The guard is from England. He is *English*.
The King is from Boonland. He is *Boonese*.

What nationality are people from these countries?

GROUP 1 France, The Netherlands
GROUP 2 Japan, China, Portugal
GROUP 3 Iraq, Pakistan, Bangladesh
GROUP 4 Sweden, Spain, Poland, Denmark, Finland
GROUP 5 Mexico, Sri Lanka, Cuba
GROUP 6 Italy, Bolivia, Canada, Egypt, Norway, Peru
GROUP 7 Greece, Thailand, Iceland

Why are the countries in groups?

3 The restaurant

Scene	The customers' home in London (I)
	A restaurant in London (II–V)
Characters	Customer A
	Customer B
	The manager of the restaurant
	Manfred Schmidt, a Spanish guitarist

I   *A and B are at home.*

Customer A   Let's go to a restaurant tonight.
Customer B   OK.
Customer A   Somewhere different.
Customer B   All right. Let's have a look in the newspaper.

           B opens the newspaper.

Customer B   Er . . . Cinemas . . . Theatres . . . Restaurants. Ooh, this sounds nice. (*Reading:*) 'London's newest restaurant. The *Trattoria Romantica*.'
Customer A   It sounds good.
Customer B   'The *Trattoria Romantica*. The best French restaurant in London.'
Customer A   French?
Customer B   Yes.

Customer A	'*Trattoria Romantica*' sounds Italian.
Customer B	It says *French* here.
Customer A	What else does it say?
Customer B	'Open every evening —'
Customer A	Good.
Customer B	'— from 7.30 to 7.45.'
Customer A	What? Fifteen minutes?
Customer B	It must be a mistake.
Customer A	I hope so. Anything else?
Customer B	Yes. 'Music every evening —'
Customer A	Good.
Customer B	'— from our Spanish guitarist —'
Customer A	Spanish guitarist?
Customer B	'— Manfred Schmidt.'
Customer A	Manfred Schmidt?!
Customer B	Yes. Oh, and there's a picture of the manager.
Customer A	What's his name?
Customer B	Stavros Papadopoulos.
Customer A	Stavros Papadopoulos?
Customer B	Yes.
Customer A	But that's a *Greek* name.
Customer B	Yes.
Customer A	So it's an *Italian* restaurant, serving *French* food . . . The *Spanish* guitarist has got a *German* name . . . And the manager's *Greek*.
Customer B	That's right. It sounds very international. Let's try it.
Customer A	All right.

II   *Later. They arrive at the restaurant.*

Customer B	Well, here we are — the *Trattoria Romantica*.
Customer A	There's no-one here. (*Calling:*) Hallo?

The manager appears. He is not very friendly.

Manager	Yes?
Customer A	Oh, good evening. Is this the *Trattoria Romantica*?
Manager	I don't know. I only work here.
Customer A	Pardon?
Manager	Yes, yes, yes. This is the *Trattoria Romantica*, but we're closed for lunch.
Customer B	Closed for lunch? But it's nine o'clock.
Manager	In that case, we're closed for breakfast.
Customer B	It's nine o'clock in the *evening*.
Manager	(*Friendly:*) Yes, of course it is. Just a little joke. Allow me to introduce myself. I am Stavros Papadopoulos, the manager of the *Trattoria Romantica*. What can I do for you?
Customer B	We'd like a table for two, please.
Manager	Have you got a reservation?
Customer B	Er . . . No.

Manager	Ah. That's a problem.
Customer A	But the restaurant is empty.
Manager	Is it? Oh, yes. Er . . . a table for two. . .

He looks around the restaurant.

Manager	Here you are — a lovely table for two.
Customer A	Thank you.

III **A and B sit down at the table.**

Manager	Is everything all right?
Customer B	Yes, thank you.

Manager	Good. That's £12.50, please.
Customer B	What?
Manager	£12.50.
Customer A	What for?
Manager	For the chairs.
Customer A	The chairs?!
Manager	Yes — £6.25 each.
Customer B	There must be some mistake.
Manager	Oh, sorry — £6.30. That's £12.60 altogether. And of course £37 for the table.
Customer B	£37 for the table?!
Manager	That's . . . er . . . £49.60 altogether.
Customer A	Look here —
Manager	Service not included.
Customer B	Service?!
Manager	Would you like to pay separately or together?
Customer A	Look — we don't *want* the table or the chairs.
Manager	Oh, you want to sit on the floor.
Customer B	No, we don't want to *take* them *away*.
Manager	That's good. We don't have a take-away service.
Customer B	We want to sit here and eat something.

Manager	Eat something?
Customer B	Yes.
Manager	Ah.
Customer B	Can we see the menu, please?
Manager	Er . . . yes. There you are.

IV

He gives them a very small menu.

Customer A	It's a very small menu.
Manager	It's a very small restaurant. What would you like?
Customer B	(*Looking at the menu:*) Let's see . . . (*Reading:*) 'Egg and chips. Double egg and chips. Double egg and double chips.'
Customer A	Um . . . Isn't this a *French* restaurant?
Manager	Oh, yes. Sorry. Give me the menu.

The manager takes the menu.

Manager	Thank you. Have you got a pencil?
Customer B	Here you are.

B gives the manager a pencil.

Manager	Thank you.

He writes on the menu.

Manager	There — a French menu.

He gives the menu back to B.

Customer B	(*Reading:*) 'Oeuf et pommes frites. Deux oeufs et pommes frites. Deux oeufs et deux pommes frites.'

B puts the menu on the table.

Customer A	What if you don't like eggs?
Manager	Have the chips.
Customer B	What if you don't like chips?
Manager	Have the eggs.
Customer A	What if you don't like eggs or chips?
Manager	Have a sandwich.
Customer B	A sandwich?
Manager	Yes. I've got one here in my pocket.

He puts a sandwich on the table.

Customer B	Thank you. Er . . . what's *in* this sandwich?
Manager	Sand.
Customer A } **Customer B** }	Sand?!
Manager	Yes, sand. That's why it's called a sandwich — because of the sand which is inside it.

V

Customer A	(*To B:*) Come on, let's go.
Manager	What's the matter? You're not going already are you?

Customer B	Yes.
Manager	Why?
Customer A	Because this must be the worst restaurant in London.
Manager	No, it isn't.
Customer B	Isn't it?
Manager	No. I've got another one round the corner. It's much worse than this one. Anyway, people don't come here for the food.
Customer A	I'm not surprised.
Manager	No, they come here for the music.
Customer B	The music?
Manager	Yes. Allow me to present Manfred Schmidt and his Spanish guitar.

Manfred comes in with his guitar.

Manfred	Olé! Guten Abend, meine Damen und Herren!

Customer A	Stavros?
Manager	Yes?
Customer A	What can Manfred play?
Manager	Anything you like.
Customer A	Really?
Manager	Yes, anything at all.
Customer A	Good. Tell him to play football.
Manager	Football? What do you mean?
Customer A	We're leaving. Goodbye.
Manager	Oh, goodbye. Do come again. Don't forget to tell your friends!

A and B leave the restaurant.

Manager	That's the trouble with English people, Manfred.
Manfred	What's that, Stavros?
Manager	They don't know a good restaurant when they see one.

About the sketch

Choose the right words

I 1 The name of the restaurant sounds *French/Italian/Greek*.
   2 The guitarist's name sounds *English/Spanish/German*.

II 3 The manager's family name is *Schmidt/Papadopoulos*.
   4 The restaurant *seems/does not seem* very popular.

III 5 Service *is/is not* included at the Trattoria Romantica.
    6 The Trattoria Romantica *has/does not have* a take-away service.

IV 7 There is *a lot/not much* on the menu.
   8 The Trattoria Romantica *serves/does not serve* sandwiches.

V 9 The Trattoria Romantica *is/is not* the worst restaurant in London.
  10 Manfred *speaks/does not speak* English.

Communicating

1 Choosing a restaurant

Look at these lines from the sketch:

The Trattoria Romantica. The best French restaurant in London. Open every evening from 7.30 to 7.45.

Practise in pairs with this information:

The Lotus Garden	Chinese	257, Old Brompton Road	Open: 1–3, 6–12
The Village	Indian	541, Kings Road	Open: 12–3, 6–11
La Cucaracha	Mexican	12, Greek Street	Open: 12.30–2.30, 6.30–11.30
The Busabong	Thai	331, Fulham Road	Open: 1–3.30, 7–12

A has the information, and begins:
This sounds nice. The Lotus Garden.

B asks these questions, and A answers:
What kind of restaurant is it?
Where is it?
When is it open?

Finally, B decides, and says: *Let's try (NAME OF RESTAURANT).*

2 Ordering in a restaurant

MENU

STARTERS
Tomato soup
Orange juice
Prawn cocktail

MAIN DISHES
Roast beef
Grilled chicken
Fish pie

DESSERTS
Ice cream (chocolate, vanilla or strawberry)
Apple pie

In threes, practise arriving at a restaurant and ordering from the menu.
One person is the waiter, and two people are the customers.
Use these expressions when you arrive and sit down:

A table for two, please.

(WAITER) Have you got a reservation?

Can we see the menu, please?

And these expressions when you are ready to order:

(WAITER) What would you like?

The . . ., please. And then the . . .
I'll have the . . ., please. And then the . . .
I'd like the . . ., please. And then the . . .

3 Asking for explanations

If you do not understand something on the menu, you can ask the waiter to explain:

> Can / Could you tell me what this is, please?...

Ask and answer in pairs, about these dishes:

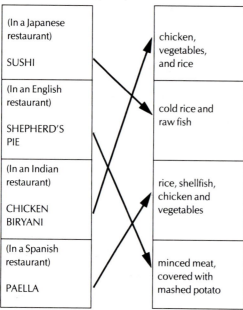

(In a Japanese restaurant) SUSHI	chicken, vegetables, and rice
(In an English restaurant) SHEPHERD'S PIE	cold rice and raw fish
(In an Indian restaurant) CHICKEN BIRYANI	rice, shellfish, chicken and vegetables
(In a Spanish restaurant) PAELLA	minced meat, covered with mashed potato

If you are vegetarian, these questions are useful:

> Have you got anything without meat?
> Has ... got meat in it?
> Is there any meat in ...?

Question time

Here are the answers to ten questions about the people, places and things in the sketch. What are the questions?

1. ....? No, it's new.
2. ....? French.
3. ....? Every evening from 7.30 to 7.45.
4. ....? A Spanish guitarist.
5. ....? Stavros Papadopoulos.
6. ....? Greek.
7. ....? Because it's a very small restaurant.
8. ....? No, he doesn't speak French very well.
9. ....? No, he's got *two*.
10. ....? Because of the sand which is inside it.

Reading: Restaurant advertisements

These advertisements are for restaurants in London. Look at them and answer the questions.

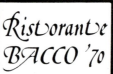

Ristorante BACCO '70

Fully licensed
Italian Restaurant
Open 12 - 3pm &
6pm - 1am
Closed Sundays

___

10 Old Compton Street
London W1

01-437 2739

CHOYS

酒樓 中 英

For Excellent Chinese Cuisine
Fully Licensed
Open Daily. Noon - Midnight
Including Sundays
172 Kings Rd, Chelsea
(352 9085 or 352 0505)

寿司・日本料理 Sakura JAPANESE RESTAURANT

9 Hanover Street, W.1.
2 min from Oxford Circus tube station
(off Regent Street)
We are open 7 days a week
Lunch: 12.00am 3.00pm
Snack: 3.00pm 5.00pm
Dinner: 5.30pm (Last order 10.00 please)
An extensive menu including many
world famous Japanese dishes like
'Sukiyaki' and 'Tempura'. Your
satisfaction is our pleasure.

Tel: 629 2961   629 3116

Step in and experience an exotic Orient in our relaxing and friendly restaurant.

LIVE ENTERTAINMENT

DON PEPE
Spanish Restaurant

"A LITTLE CORNER OF
SPAIN IN LONDON"

OPEN
12-3 & 6.30-12.15
(last orders) Mon-Sat.
12-2 & 7.00-10.15 (last orders) Sun.

99 FRAMPTON ST, LONDON NW8
01-262 3834   &   01-723 9749

24

1 Each restaurant serves a different kind
   of food. What are the different kinds?
2 Which restaurants have music?
3 Which restaurants are open on
   Sundays?
4 What is the telephone number for
   reservations at the Indian restaurant?

Writing: An advertisement

Look at this advertisement for the *Trattoria
Romantica*:

London's newest French restaurant

The TRATTORIA ROMANTICA

17, Stone Street, London SW1

The best French restaurant in London!
OPEN EVERY EVENING: 7.30–7.45

Our specialities include: Coq au vin,
Spaghetti alle vongole,
Boeuf bourgignon, Egg and chips,
Knackwurst, Taramasalata

MUSIC EVERY EVENING FROM
OUR SPANISH GUITARIST,
MANFRED SCHMIDT

MANAGER:
STAVROS PAPADOPOULOS
For reservations, telephone 100–0001

Invent a restaurant and write a similar
advertisement for it. It can be funny or serious.

In your own words

Re-enact the sketch in your own words,
without reading from the text. Do it in short
sections. These words will remind you.

I	II	III	IV	V
newspaper T.R open music manager	closed a table for two	chairs/table eat something menu	egg + chips a sandwich	going food/music Goodbye!

Word puzzle

Put the correct words in the vertical columns.
Then read the expression in the horizontal
box.

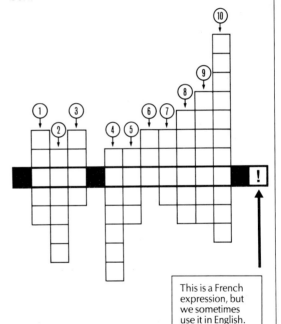

This is a French
expression, but
we sometimes
use it in English.
It means 'I hope
you enjoy the
meal'.

1 'We'd like a .... for two, please.'
2 'Here you are — a .... table for two.'
3 'Can we see the...., please?'
4 At the *Trattoria Romantica*, the .... is
   Stavros Papadopoulos.
5 The *Trattoria Romantica* is .... every
   evening.
6 If service is not included, you can
   leave a.....
7 The person who cooks the food in a
   restaurant is the.....

25

8 A man who serves you in a restaurant is a . . . . .

9 'Is . . . . included?'

10 'Have you got a . . . . ?'

Extra!

English words from other languages

The sketch was about the Trattoria Romantica. 'Trattoria' is an Italian word, meaning a kind of restaurant. You can now find it in English dictionaries.

Here are some English words. Do you know which languages they come from? If not, follow the lines.

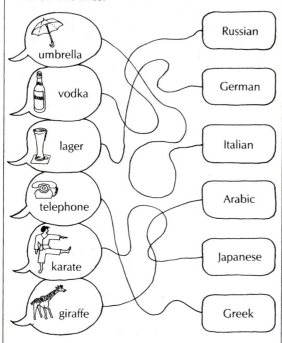

Are there any English words in *your* language?

4 The passport office

Scene	A passport office in Britain
Characters	The passport office clerk A man who wants a passport The man's girl-friend

I   *The clerk is working at her desk. The man comes in and coughs twice.*

Clerk   Oh, good morning. Can I help you?

Man   Yes. Have you got any passports?

Clerk   Yes, we have.

Man   Oh, good. The shop next door hasn't got any. I'd like twenty, please.

Clerk   Twenty?

Man   Yes. All different colours.

Clerk   I'm sorry. That's impossible.

Man   All right. All the *same* colour.

Clerk   No, no — it's impossible to have twenty passports.

Man   Is it?

Clerk   Yes. You can only have one.

Man	Oh, all right. One passport, please.	

He offers some money.

Clerk	Just a minute. It isn't as easy as that. You have to answer some questions.
Man	Oh.
Clerk	What kind of passport do you want?
Man	What kind of passport?
Clerk	Yes.
Man	A big round yellow one.
Clerk	We've only got small blue rectangular ones. When I say 'What kind?', I mean: How long?
Man	How long?
Clerk	How long? Five years? Ten years?
Man	I want it *today.*
Clerk	No, I mean: How long do you want it to last?
Man	How long do I want it to last?
Clerk	Yes.
Man	A hundred years.
Clerk	A hundred years?!
Man	Yes.
Clerk	You can't have a passport for a hundred years.
Man	Why not?
Clerk	Er . . . I don't know. All right — a passport for a hundred years. Now, we have to fill in this form. Er . . . Do sit down.
Man	Oh, thank you.

He sits down

II	**Clerk**	Now . . . first question. Name.
	Man	William Shakespeare.
	Clerk	William Shakespeare?
	Man	Yes.
	Clerk	Is that your name?
	Man	No, but it's a very nice name.
	Clerk	Yes, but what's *your* name?
	Man	Oh, *my* name. Sorry.
	Clerk	Well, what is it?
	Man	Smith.
	Clerk	(*Writing*:) Smith.
	Man	(*In a high voice*:) That's right. Smith. S-M-I-T-H.
	Clerk	Pardon?
	Man	Smith, that's right.
	Clerk	And what's is your first name, Mr Smith?
	Man	(*In a high voice*:) Charles.
	Clerk	Pardon?
	Man	Charles.

Clerk (*Writing:*) Charles.

Man (*In a low voice:*) That's right.

III ***The clerk is puzzled.***

Clerk Mr Smith?

Man (*In a high voice:*) Yes?

Clerk There's something rather strange about the way you speak.

Man Is there?

Clerk Yes. When I say your family name —

Man Smith.

Clerk Yes, Smith —

Man (*In a high voice:*) Yes?

Clerk Your voice goes up.

Man Does it?

Clerk Yes. And when I say your first name —

Man Charles.

Clerk Yes, Charles —

Man (*In a low voice:*) Yes?

Clerk Your voice goes down.

Man Er . . . yes, it's true. It's a very big problem when I'm having a conversation.

Clerk That's right.

Man But there is a solution.

Clerk	What is it?
Man	You can call me by a different name.
Clerk	A different name?
Man	Yes. Then we can have a normal conversation.
Clerk	Oh, good. What name would you like?
Man	Brunhilde.
Clerk	What?
Man	Call me Brunhilde.
Clerk	Brunhilde —
Man	— Schwarzkopf.
Clerk	I beg your pardon?
Man	Schwarzkopf. Brunhilde Schwarzkopf. Just write it down.
Clerk	(*Suspicious*:) Write it down?
Man	Oh, yes — you must write it down. You see, if I see my *real* name on a piece of paper, my voice goes funny. (*In a high voice*:) Look, there it is —

He taps the form.

Man	(*In a high voice*:) — Quick! Smith! Cross it out! Cross it out!
Clerk	Right.

The clerk crosses out his name.

Man	That's better.
Clerk	(*Writing*:) Now . . . Brunhilde Schwarzkopf. Well, Miss Schwarzkopf, there are one or two more questions. Er . . . Question 2: Address.
Man	Pardon?
Clerk	Address.
Man	No, it isn't.
Clerk	What?
Man	It isn't a dress. I'm not wearing a dress. It's a raincoat.
Clerk	No, no — address, address!
Man	No, no — a raincoat, a raincoat!
Clerk	Look — where do you *live*?
Man	Oh, where do I *live*?
Clerk	Yes.
Man	Round the corner.
Clerk	Can you be more exact?
Man	Er . . . *just* round the corner.
Clerk	Brunhilde! What is your address?
Man	OK, OK. My address is 14 . . . Brunhilde Street.
Clerk	(*Writing*:) 14, Brun — Ah! That means 14 *Smith* Street, doesn't it?
Man	(*In a high voice*:) No — 14, *Charles* Street.
Clerk	14, Charles Street.
Man	(*In a low voice*:) That's right.

IV is marked to the left of the Clerk line beginning "(*Writing*:) Now . . . Brunhilde Schwarzkopf."

V

Clerk	Now . . . nationality.

Man	Er . . . just write 'British'.
Clerk	*Are* you British?
Man	It doesn't matter. Just write 'British'.
Clerk	Brunhilde, are you or are you not British?
Man	That is a very good question.
Clerk	And what is the answer?
Man	It's a bit complicated.
Clerk	All right, then. Let's start at the beginning. Where were you born?
Man	I don't remember.
Clerk	You don't remember.
Man	No.
Clerk	Why not?
Man	I was very young at the time.
Clerk	Well, what about your father and mother?
Man	They were older than me.
Clerk	Brunhilde! Tell me about your mother.
Man	She was very nice . . . tall, with a long black beard.
Clerk	Your mother?
Man	Oh no, that was my father. My mother was much shorter — and she didn't have a long black beard. She had a *short* black beard.
Clerk	(*Angry:*) All right! That's enough! I don't want to hear any more! Just take your passport —
Man	Oh, thank you.

She gives him a passport.

Clerk	— put a photograph in it, and go anywhere in the world. But *don't* come back here!

She leaves the office.

Man	Hmm . . . A British passport, in the name of Brunhilde Schwarzkopf. Excellent. Brunhilde!

His girl-friend, Brunhilde, comes in.

Brunhilde	Ja?
Man	I've got a passport for you.
Brunhilde	Ja?
Man	Now we can go anywhere in the world.
Brunhilde	Ja!
Man	What about a holiday in the sun?
Brunhilde	Ja!
Man	(*To himself:*) She doesn't understand a word I say.
Brunhilde	Ja!

About the sketch

Correct these sentences.

I   1 British passports are small, yellow and rectangular.
    2 You can have twenty passports.
II 3 The man's name was Shakespeare.
    4 His first name was Smith.
III 5 He had a high voice all the time.
    6 Brunhilde Schwarzkopf was his real name.
IV 7 His house was a long way from the Passport Office.
    8 His address was 14, Smith Street.
V   9 His father had a short black beard.
    10 Brunhilde was British.

Communicating

1   Asking for and giving personal information (informal)

Can you answer all these questions about yourself?

1	What's your name?
2	What's your address? Where do you live?
3	What's your telephone number?
4	Where are you from?
5	When were you born?
6	Where were you born?

Ask and answer in pairs.

2   Asking for and giving personal information (formal)

Look at these lines from the sketch:

First question. Name.
What is your name? What is your first name?
Question 2. Address.
What is your address?
Now ... Nationality.

Practise in pairs, asking and answering these questions:

1a	What is your family name?
b	What is your first name?
2	What is your address?
3	What is your telephone number?
4	What nationality are you?
5	What is your date of birth?
6	What is your place of birth?

One person is an official (A), and one person is a traveller (B). A asks the questions and writes down B's answers; B spells the words when necessary. Afterwards, B checks A's spelling.

Question time

Here are the answers to ten questions about the sketch. What are the questions?

1	....?	Only one.
2	....?	Small, blue and rectangular.
3	....?	Smith.
4	....?	Charles
5	....?	14, Charles Street.
6	....?	Just round the corner from the Passport Office.
7	....?	Tall, with a long black beard.
8	....?	Brunhilde.
9	....?	Schwarzkopf.
10	....?	No, she was probably German.

Reading: Completing a text

Read this text about the people in the sketch, and put in the missing words.

The man's real ... was Charles Smith. There was something rather ... about his ...: sometimes it was ... and sometimes it ... low. He lives just round the ... from the Passport Office. The name of his ... is the same as his ... name: *Charles* Street. He ... at Number 14. He is probably British, and his ... is probably ... . Her first ... is Brunhilde and her ... name is Schwarzkopf. Mr Smith's ... was tall and he ... a long ... beard. Mr Smith was certainly a strange customer for the Passport Office clerk.

Writing: Filling in a form

Fill in this form about yourself.

FAMILY NAME:	....
FIRST NAME(S):	....
DATE OF BIRTH:	....
PLACE OF BIRTH:	....
NATIONALITY:	....
HEIGHT:	....
COLOUR OF EYES:	....
COLOUR OF HAIR:	....
ADDRESS:	....
TEL. NO.:	....

Note: In Britain, when dates are written in numbers, they look like this:

2.11.48   or   2/11/48

(= 2nd November 1948 — first the *day*, then the *month*, then the *year*).

You can also write dates in these ways:

Nov.2.48   Nov.2nd 1948

November 2nd 1948

In your own words

Re-enact the sketch in your own words, without reading from the text. Do it in short sections. These words will remind you.

I	II	III	IV	V
passports (20/1) What kind? How long?	name First name	up / down solution: Brunhilde	address	nationality father/ mother photograph

Word puzzle

There are fifteen words from the sketch in this grid, either in this direction ➡ , this direction ⬇ or this direction ↘ . Can you find them? (Some letters are used in more than one word.)

P	N	O	F	F	I	C	E	B	A
B	A	D	D	R	E	S	S	R	H
R	M	S	L	F	O	R	M	U	O
I	E	P	S	K	A	Y	U	N	L
T	T	N	U	P	C	M	V	H	I
I	P	A	N	M	O	T	I	I	D
S	B	A	L	X	L	R	R	L	A
H	I	T	P	L	O	K	T	D	Y
K	G	E	C	E	U	D	F	E	W
W	O	R	L	D	R	Q	A	L	N

Extra!

Famous people

Here are passport photographs of some famous English people. Unfortunately, the wrong names are under them. Put the names with the correct photographs.

William Shakespeare

Queen Victoria

Prince Charles

Princess Diana

Margaret Thatcher

Charles Dickens

Lord Nelson

Winston Churchill

5 Fire practice

Scene   A fire station

Characters   The fire chief
Boggins ⎫
Coggins ⎬ new recruits to
Foggins ⎭ the Fire Service

I

The fire chief is in the fire station. Someone knocks loudly at the door.

Fire chief   Come in!

Foggins comes in.

Foggins   Don't panic!!!
Fire chief   Can I help you?
Foggins   Yes. I want a job.
Fire chief   You want a job.
Foggins   Yes. I want to be a fireman.
Fire chief   You want to be a fireman.
Foggins   That's right.
Fire chief   Why do you want to be a fireman?

Foggins	Well, I like *smashing* things — like doors, and windows, and tables —
Fire chief	Well, I don't know . . .
Foggins	Please!
Fire chief	What's your name?
Foggins	Foggins.
Fire chief	Foggins?
Foggins	Yeah, 'Smasher' Foggins.
Fire chief	Well, Mr Foggins, do you know anything about the Fire Service? For example, what is the most important thing in a fireman's equipment?
Foggins	What is . . . the meaning of the word 'equipment'?
Fire chief	Equipment . . . you know . . . *things*. What is the most important thing a fireman's got?
Foggins	His axe.
Fire chief	Wrong.
Foggins	What is it, then?
Fire chief	His telephone.
Foggins	His telephone?
Fire chief	Yes, Foggins.
Foggins	You can't smash doors with a telephone.
Fire chief	That's right, Foggins. But when this telephone rings, someone is in trouble. When this telephone rings, someone needs help. When this telephone rings, someone needs the Fire Service.

The telephone rings. The fire chief answers it.

Fire chief	Not now, I'm busy.

He puts down the telephone.

Fire chief	(*To Foggins*:) So, Foggins, the most important part of our equipment is —
Foggins	— the telephone.
Fire chief	Right! OK, Foggins, I've got an idea. You can do fire practice today with the new firemen. Would you like to meet them?
Foggins	Yes, please.
Fire chief	Good. Boggins!

Boggins comes in.

Boggins	Sir!
Fire chief	Coggins!

Coggins comes in.

Coggins	Sir!
Fire chief	Foggins, this is Boggins and Coggins. Boggins, Coggins and Foggins. Coggins, Foggins and Boggins. Right — fire practice. Question 1. Boggins!
Boggins	Yes, sir!
Fire chief	Where do most fires start?

II

Boggins	In a box of matches, sir.
Fire chief	No. Coggins?
Coggins	Don't know, sir.
Fire chief	Foggins?
Foggins	What was the question again?
Fire chief	Where do most fires start?
Foggins	At the fire station.
Fire chief	No, Foggins. The answer is: In your house.
Foggins	What?!
Fire chief	Yes, Foggins. In your house.
Foggins	Well, I'm not staying here, then.

Foggins goes towards the door.

Fire chief	Where are you going?
Foggins	I'm going home.
Fire chief	Why?
Foggins	You said most fires start in *my* house.
Fire chief	Not in *your* house, Foggins. In *everybody's* house.
Boggins **Coggins** **Foggins**	What?!

They panic. The fire chief blows his whistle.

Fire chief	Look — don't panic. It's just an expression. It means 'houses in general'.
Boggins **Coggins** **Foggins**	Oh.

III	**Fire chief**	Now, Question 2. Coggins!
	Coggins	Sir!
	Fire chief	What should you do if there's a fire in your house?
	Coggins	Go next door, sir.
	Fire chief	No, Coggins. You should call the Fire Service.
	Coggins	Ooh, good idea, sir.
	Fire chief	And that's where *we* start work. Because the most important part of our equipment is —
	Boggins **Coggins** **Foggins**	— the telephone!

Fire chief	Right! Now, telephone practice. Boggins!
Boggins	Sir!
Fire chief	Give the telephone to Coggins.
Boggins	Sir!

Boggins gives the telephone to Coggins.

Fire chief	Coggins!

Coggins	Sir?
Fire chief	*You* are the telephone. Foggins!
Foggins	What?
Fire chief	*You* are the telephone bell.
Foggins	What do you mean?
Fire chief	When I blow my whistle, make a ringing noise. Telephone practice — begin!

The fire chief blows his whistle. Foggins makes a noise like an ambulance.

Fire chief	Not an *ambulance*, Foggins — a telephone! Start again.

The fire chief blows his whistle again.

Foggins	Ring, ring. Ring, ring.

Fire chief	Boggins.
Foggins	Ring, ring.
Boggins	Yes, sir?
Foggins	Ring, ring.
Fire chief	The telephone's ringing.
Foggins	Ring, ring.
Boggins	No, it isn't sir. It's Foggins, sir. He's going 'Ring, ring', sir.
Foggins	Ring, ring.
Boggins	There you are, sir.
Fire chief	Boggins, answer the telephone!
Boggins	All right, sir.

Boggins picks up the telephone.

Foggins	Ring, ring. Ring, ring.
Fire chief	Foggins!
Foggins	Ring — What?
Fire chief	Stop it!

Foggins	Brrrrrrr.	
Boggins	Nobody there, sir.	
IV	**Fire chief**	Let's start again.

Boggins puts down the telephone.

Fire chief	Telephone practice — begin!

The fire chief blows his whistle again.

Foggins	Ring, ring. Ring, ring.

Boggins picks up the telephone.

Boggins	Hallo?
Fire chief	Fire station.
Boggins	Oh, hallo, fire station!
Fire chief	No, Boggins! You *are* the fire station.
Boggins	Oh, yes. Sorry, sir. Hallo? Fire station.
Fire chief	(*In a high voice*:) Help! Help!
Boggins	Is something wrong, sir?
Fire chief	No, Boggins. I am an old lady. I am an old lady, and my house is on fire. That's why I'm calling the fire station.
Boggins	I see, sir.
Fire chief	Continue.
Boggins	Hallo, old lady. Can I help you?
Fire chief	(*In a high voice*:) Yes. There's a fire in my kitchen.
Boggins	OK. We're on our way.

Boggins puts down the telephone.

Boggins	Was that all right, sir?
Fire chief	Boggins, where is the fire?
Boggins	In the old lady's kitchen, sir.
Fire chief	Where is the old lady's kitchen?
Boggins	In the old lady's house, sir.
Fire chief	Where is the house?
Boggins	Oh, dear!

V	***The telephone rings.***

Fire chief	Foggins, stop making that noise.
Foggins	It's not me — it's the telephone.
Fire chief	Is it? Oh, right. Coggins!
Coggins	Sir?
Fire chief	Answer the telephone.
Coggins	Sir!

Coggins answers the telephone.

Coggins	Yes . . . Yes . . . Yes . . . Yes . . . Yes . . . Yes. OK, we're on our way.

Coggins puts down the telephone

Fire chief	Very good, Coggins. What is it?
Coggins	A fire, sir.
Fire chief	Did you get the name?
Coggins	Yes, sir.
Fire chief	Did you get the address?
Coggins	Yes, sir.
Fire chief	Do you know how to get there?
Coggins	Yes, sir.
Fire chief	Right. Get in line and don't panic. This is your first fire. Coggins, where's the fire?
Coggins	In Railway Street, sir.
Fire chief	In Rail — In Railway Street?!
Coggins	Yes, sir.
Fire chief	What number?
Coggins	Number 44, sir.
Fire chief	What?! Quick! Hurry up! Get out of here and *do* something!
Foggins	All right, al! right — you said 'Don't panic'.

Fire chief	Never mind 'Don't panic'. Panic!
Boggins	What's the matter, sir? It's just a house on fire.
Fire chief	Yes, but it's *my* house! Panic!

They panic.

About the sketch

Answer these questions.

I   1 Why did Foggins want to be a fireman?
    2 What is the most important part of a fireman's equipment?
II 3 What was Question 1 in the fire practice?
    4 Why did Foggins say 'I'm going home'?
III 5 What was Question 2 in the fire practice?
    6 Why did Foggins say 'Ring, ring'?
IV 7 Why did the fire chief speak in a high voice?
    8 What mistake did Boggins make?
V 9 Where was the fire?
  10 Why did the fire chief panic?

Communicating

1 Giving practical hints

Look at these lines from the sketch:

> What should you do if there's a fire in your house?
> Go next door, sir.
> No, Coggins. You should call the Fire Service.
> Ooh, good idea, sir.

Give practical hints for the problems below. Ask and answer in pairs.

— You're on holiday abroad and you lose your passport.
— You're in a taxi and you discover that you have no money.
— You're lost in a strange town.
— You see someone stealing a car.

2 Talking on the telephone

The new firemen in the sketch had some problems with the telephone. In Section **IV**, Boggins made a mistake, and in Section **V**, Coggins avoided the mistake. Read Sections **IV** and **V** again.

Here are some useful expressions for talking on the telephone:

> Can I speak to (NAME), please?
> Hold on.
> Speaking.
> Hallo, (NAME).   It's (NAME).

Read this start of a telephone conversation, and put the expressions in the right places.

X Hallo? 5-4-3-2-1.
Y Hallo. . . . . Z, please?
X . . . .

40

Z comes to the phone.

Z Hallo?
X Z?
Z . . . .
X Hallo, Z. . . . X.

Practise the start of the conversation in groups of three, and continue it as you like.

3 Giving directions

Look at these lines from the sketch:

> Do you know how to get there?
> Yes, sir.

Say how to get from the fire station to Railway Street. Use the map below. These expressions are useful:

> Go straight on.
> Turn left./Turn right.
> Take the first/second/third on the left/right.

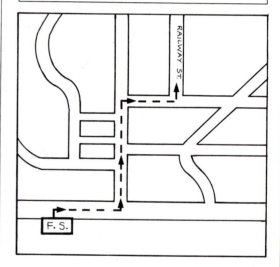

Question time

Here are the answers to ten questions about the sketch. What are the questions?

1 . . . . ? Doors, tables and windows.
2 . . . . ? The telephone.
3 . . . . ? Coggins and Boggins.
4 . . . . ? 'Houses in general'.
5 . . . . ? You should call the Fire Service.
6 . . . . ? An ambulance.
7 . . . . ? In the old lady's kitchen.
8 . . . . ? In Railway Street.
9 . . . . ? 44.
10 . . . . ? The fire chief's.

Reading: A notice

The sketch is not serious, but here is some serious advice about fire prevention. Read it and answer the questions.

FIRE PREVENTION IN THE OFFICE

Fires don't just happen. There is always a cause.

Remember:
Use ashtrays – not the waste-paper-basket.
Switch off machines at night and remove the plugs.
Don't place paper, towels or clothing near portable fires.

Fire precautions

Read the fire instructions NOW.
Find out where the escape routes are.

If it is necessary to pass through smoke:
– inhale as little as possible
– keep near the floor if the smoke is dense.
Don't use the lift.

1 What do these words mean?
portable, inhale, dense
2 Why does the notice say 'Don't use the lift'?
3 Where is the fire precautions notice in your school?

Writing: Telephone messages

Read this telephone conversation, the notes and the message:

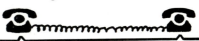

TOM	Hallo – is Sue there?
ANN	No, I'm sorry, she's out.
TOM	Can I leave a message?
ANN	Yes, of course.
TOM	It's Tom here. Can you ask Sue to call me back this evening? My number's 100–1001. I need to talk to her about tomorrow's tennis match.
ANN	OK, I've got that.
TOM	Thanks a lot. Bye.
ANN	Bye.

Tom
100 – 1001
tennis match

PHONE MESSAGE

Sue - Tom called this afternoon.
Please call him back this evening (100-1001).
It's about tomorrow's tennis match.

Practise in pairs:
A 'telephones' and leaves a message for someone;
B makes notes during the phone conversation.
Then, B 'telephones' and leaves a message for someone;
A makes notes during the phone conversation.
Then, each person writes a message from his/her notes.

In your own words

Re-enact the sketch in your own words, without reading from the text. Do it in short sections. These words will remind you.

I
fireman
Foggins
equipment:
telephone

II
Q.1:
fires start?
house

III
Q.2.
telephone
practice
Ring, ring!

IV
old lady
fire
kitchen

V
Yes...yes...
address
Panic!

Word puzzle

Put the words in the right places. All the words appeared in the sketch.

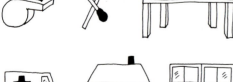

Extra!

Telephone operator services

In the sketch, the fire chief said:

> The most important part of our equipment is the telephone.

In Britain, you telephone 999 for the Fire Service.
Look at this information:

Operator services : Inland

SOS-Emergency calls 999
Fire, Police, Ambulance, Coastguard
(Ask for the emergency service you want)

Operator, difficulties and enquiries
Operator 100
Difficulty in obtaining a dialled call 100

Fault repair service 151
(Telephone out of order or broken)

Telegrams
International telegrams 193

Which numbers do you dial for these services in your country?

6 The bus stop

Scene	A bus stop
Characters	An old lady
	A robber
	A student
	A policeman

I
The robber is waiting at the bus stop.
The old lady joins him.

Old lady	Excuse me.
Robber	Yes?
Old lady	The 44.
Robber	The 44?
Old lady	Yes. The Number 44 bus. Does it stop here?
Robber	I don't know.

He looks at the notice on the bus stop.

Robber	Um . . . 39 . . . 40 . . . 41 . . . 42 . . . 43 . . . 45. No, it doesn't.
Old lady	Pardon?
Robber	The 44 doesn't stop here.

Old lady	Oh, good.
Robber	Pardon?
Old lady	I said 'Oh, good'. I'm very pleased.
Robber	What do you mean?
Old lady	I don't want to catch a 44.

She laughs. The robber is not pleased, and stands with his back to her.

Old lady	Excuse me again.
Robber	Yes?
Old lady	The 46.
Robber	The 46?
Old lady	Yes. The Number 46 bus. Does it stop here?
Robber	Do you want to catch a 46?
Old lady	Um . . . Yes.

The robber looks at the notice again.

Robber	42, 43, 45 . . . 45A, 45B, 45C, 45D . . . 46. Yes. Yes, the 46 stops here.
Old lady	Oh, good.
Robber	Ah, here comes a 46 now.

A bus passes very fast.

Old lady	It didn't stop!
Robber	I know.
Old lady	But you said the 46 stopped here. You're telling lies!
Robber	No, I'm not. That one was full. Ah, here comes another one.
Old lady	A Number 1? I don't want a Number 1. I want a Number 46.
Robber	I didn't say 'A Number 1'. I said 'Another one'. Another Number 46.
Old lady	Oh, I see.
Robber	This one will stop.

Another bus passes very fast.

Old lady	It didn't stop!
Robber	I know.

The robber stands with his back to the old lady.

II	**Old lady**	Excuse me again.
	Robber	No!
	Old lady	Pardon?
	Robber	No! The 47 doesn't stop here —
	Old lady	No, no, no.
	Robber	— or the 48, or the 49, or the 50!
	Old lady	No, you don't understand. I want to ask you a question.
	Robber	Oh, yes?
	Old lady	Are you a doctor?
	Robber	What?

Old lady	Are you a doctor?
Robber	No, I'm not.
Old lady	Are you sure you're not a doctor?
Robber	Yes, I am!
Old lady	Oh, you *are* a doctor!
Robber	No! I'm *sure* I am *not* a doctor!
Old lady	Oh. What a shame. You see, I've got this terrible pain in my back.
Robber	Well, I'm sorry. I am not a doctor. I am a robber.
Old lady	A what?
Robber	A robber — a thief.

Old lady	Teeth? No, no, not my *teeth* — my *back*. The pain's in my back. My teeth are all right.
Robber	No! I didn't say 'teeth'. I said 'thief'. Thief — robber! I am a robber. Look — here's my card.

He gives her his card.

Old lady	(*Reading:*) 'Sam Poskins. Robber. Banks a speciality.' Oh, you're a robber.
Robber	That's right.

He takes back his card.

Old lady	Help!
Robber	What's the matter?
Old lady	Police!!
Robber	Stop it!
Old lady	Murder!!!
Robber	Look — be quiet. It's all right. I rob banks. I don't rob people. And I certainly don't rob old ladies.
Old lady	Old ladies!
Robber	Yes.
Old lady	Old ladies! *I'm* not an old lady. I'm only 92.
Robber	Well, I don't care if you're 92 or 192. I am *not* going to rob you.

Old lady	I don't believe you.
Robber	What?
Old lady	I don't believe you're a robber.
Robber	Well, I *am*.
Old lady	No, no, no — impossible.
Robber	What do you mean?
Old lady	You're too small.
Robber	What do you mean — I'm 'too small'? I am *not* too small.
Old lady	Yes, you are. You're *much* too small.
Robber	No, I'm not. And anyway, I've got a gun. Look!

He takes out his gun.

Old lady	Oh, yes. You've got a gun.
Robber	That's right.
Old lady	Help!
Robber	It's all right. It's not real.
Old lady	Not real?!
Robber	No.
Old lady	You call yourself a robber! You're too small, your gun isn't real, and you can't even rob a 92-year-old lady at a bus stop!
Robber	All right, all right, all right! I'll *show* you. I will rob the next person who comes to this bus stop.
Old lady	Oh, good! . . . Look — here comes someone.
Robber	Right. Watch this.

IV   **The student stands at the bus stop, holding a book.**

Robber	Excuse me.
Student	Yes?
Robber	Put up your hands.
Student	I'm sorry. I don't speak English.
Robber	Oh. Er . . . Give me your money.
Student	What?
Robber	Your money!
Student	Money?
Robber	Yes — money, money, money!
Student	Ah! No, it's not *Money* . . . it's *Tuesday*.
Robber	No, no, no. I didn't say 'Monday'. I said 'money'. Money!
Student	No. I told you — it isn't Money, it's Tuesday. Look — it's in this book.

The student opens the book.

Student	Money, Tuesday . . .

The robber takes the book.

Robber	What is this book? 'English for all situations'. Oh, good.

V   **He looks through the book.**

Robber	Um . . . 'In a restaurant'. . . 'On a train'. . . Ah, yes — this is it: 'Unit 16. The robbery.' Good. Look — here. 'Dialogue 1: Give me your money.'

The student reads in the book too.

Student	Ah, *money*! Um . . . 'Are you trying to rob me?'
Robber	'Yes, I am.'
Student	'Are you a robber?'
Robber	'Yes, I am.'
Student	'I will call a policeman.'
Robber	'No, you won't.'
Student	'Yes, I will.'
Robber	'No, you won't.' . . . 'Policemen are like buses. You can never find one when you want one.'
Student	'No, you're wrong. There's a policeman standing behind you.'

This is true.

Robber	Ha, ha! I don't believe *that*!
Policeman	Now, what's going on here?
Robber	Oh. Er . . . well . . .

The robber, the student and the old lady all talk at once. The policeman blows his whistle.

Policeman	Right. You can all come with me to the station.
Robber	Oh, no!
Student	Oh yes — 'Unit 17: The police station.'
Old lady	Station? I don't want to catch a train. I want to catch a Number 46 bus.
Policeman	Not the *railway* station, madam — the *police* station.
Old lady	Oh, the police station! Yes, I know it. It's very near my house. Come on, everybody!

The robber, the student and the old lady walk away, all talking at once again. The policeman follows them, blowing his whistle.

About the sketch

Choose the right words.

I 1 The old lady wanted to catch a *44/45/46*.

2 The 45A *stopped/did not stop* at the bus stop.

II 3 The old lady had a problem with *her back/her teeth*.

4 'Thief' means the same as *'doctor'/'robber'*.

III 5 The robber specialized in robbing *people/banks/old ladies*.

6 The robber was not very *small/tall*.

IV 7 The student confused the words 'money' and *'Tuesday'/'Monday'*.

8 The student spoke *no English/some English/perfect English*.

V 9 The unit called 'The Robbery' was *the first/not the first* in the book.

10 At the end, they all went to *the railway station/the police station*.

Communicating

1 Finding out about bus services

In Section **I** of the sketch, the old lady asked the robber about bus services. Read Section **I** again.

Look at this information about a London bus service, and answer the questions.

BUS 60

South Croydon-Brixton Garage

	Peak hours	Between peak hours	Evenings
Mondays to Fridays	15 minutes	20 minutes	20 minutes
Saturdays	Early mornings 20 minutes	Shopping hours 15 minutes	Evenings 20 minutes
Sundays	N O S E R V I C E		

How often does the 60 run on weekdays
— at peak hours?
— between peak hours?
— in the evening?
How often does it run on Saturdays
— in the early morning?
— during shopping hours?
— in the evenings?
How often does it run on Sundays?

Now practise in pairs at the bus stop. Make dialogues like this:

A Does the 60 stop here?
B Yes, it does.
A How often does it run?
B Well, it's Saturday evening . . . er . . . every twenty minutes.
A Thank you.

It can be any day you choose.

2 Talking about language ability

In the sketch, the student said 'I'm sorry. I don't speak English'.
Here are some other useful sentences:

I'm sorry. I only speak a little English.
Could you say that again?
Could you speak more slowly?
What does '. . .' mean?

This is a useful question:

How do you say '. . .' in English?

Work in pairs. First, say what these things are in your language:

Then ask and answer like this:

A How do you say (POLICE STATION) in English?
B 'Police station'.
A Thank you.

3 Clearing up misunderstandings

There were a lot of misunderstandings in the sketch.
For example:

> A Number 1? I don't want a Number 1. I want a Number 46.
> I didn't say 'A Number 1'. I said 'Another one'. Another Number 46.
> Oh, I see.

Find the other misunderstandings in the sketch. There are six: *one each* in Sections **I**, **III**, **IV** and **V**, and *two* in Section **II**.

Question time

Here the answers to ten questions about the sketch. What are the questions?

1	....?	The 39, 40, 41, 42, 43, 45, 45A, B, C, D and 46.
2	....?	The 44, 47, 48, 49 and 50.
3	....?	Sam Poskins.
4	....?	Banks.
5	....?	Ninety-two.
6	....?	Because he was small.
7	....?	'English for all situations'.
8	....?	Unit 16.
9	....?	Unit 17.
10	....?	Near the old lady's house.

Reading: Information about bus services

Read this information about London buses, and answer the questions.

Buses

You choose your bus by the number and destination shown on the front of it. Bus numbers are indicated on the detailed London Buses map (available at Travel Information Centres and Underground stations).

At a 'Compulsory Stop' all buses stop

At a 'Request Stop' you stop the bus by raising your hand in good time

Most bus stops show which bus numbers stop there, and where the buses go. They may show a map of other stops in the area. If you are not sure which bus to catch, other people in the queue can probably help you. *Don't forget to queue up, British-style, when waiting for the bus. It's fairer for everybody.*

On most buses in Central London you pay the conductor, but on some buses (mainly in the suburbs) you enter by the front doors and pay the driver.

Most London buses are the famous red double-deckers, so climb the stairs for a splendid view!

1 Do people *queue up* at bus stops in your country?
2 Do you have *double-decker* buses in your country?
3 Do buses in your country have a driver *and* a conductor, or just one person who does both jobs?
4 Explain the difference between the two kinds of bus stop in London.

Writing: Completing a text

The old lady, the student and the robber went to the police station. Below, you can see their statements about what happened at the bus stop. The statements are not complete.

1. It was all a mistake. I . . . . bus stop. The old lady asked . . . . buses. Then she asked . . . . doctor. I . . . . robber . . . . banks . . . . people. The old lady . . . . believe me. I tried . . . . rob . . . . young lady, although I didn't want . . . . The young lady . . . . understand . . . . speak English . . . . . What a day!

2. It was all very funny. I met . . . . at the bus stop. He . . . . robber . . . . a card . . . . . Then he tried . . . . the young lady. She . . . . understand . . . . . They read . . . . from a book, and then . . . . arrived. I knew . . . . a terrible robber . . . . small . . . . real!

3. It was all very confusing. I arrived . . . . bus stop. The man . . . . my money. I . . . . English very well, and I . . . . understand him. So he . . . . Unit 16 in . . . . . Then . . . . arrived. I didn't mind really, because it was good practice for my English!

In Your Own Words

Re-enact the sketch in your own words, without reading from the text. Do it in short sections. These words will remind you.

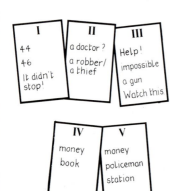

Word puzzle

Fill in the words correctly. Then add the two missing letters. You should find two of the characters from the skech in the vertical boxes.

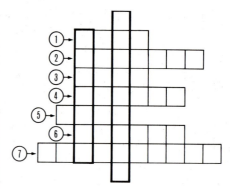

1. It didn't . . . !
2. You're . . . lies!
3. . . . . 16. The Robbery.
4. I'm *sure* I am *not* a . . .
5. The 44 doesn't stop . . . .
6. I want a . . . 46.
7. 'English for all . . .'

Extra!

Mistakes

In the sketch, the student made a mistake with the words *money* and *Monday*.
Find the mistakes in these families of words:

1. Monday, Tuesday, Wednesday, Thirsty, Friday, Saturday, Sunday
2. January, February, Mars, April, May, June, July, August, September, October, November, Remember
3. spring, summer, autumn, window
4. one, too, tree, four, five, six, seven, ate, nine, ten
5. green, yellow, read, grey, white, black, blew
6. bedroom, living-room, bathroom, chicken, dining-room
7. shirt, socks, shows, jacket, trousers, hate, coat

A ticket to Birmingham

Scene	A railway station in England
Characters	A traveller
	A British Rail employee

I   *The BR employee is sitting at a table, reading a newspaper. The traveller comes in.*

Traveller	Excuse me.
BR employee	Can I help you?
Traveller	Yes. I want a ticket.
BR employee	A ticket?
Traveller	Yes. I want a ticket to Birmingham.
BR employee	A ticket to Birmingham?
Traveller	Yes.
BR employee	Why?
Traveller	Why what?
BR employee	Why do you want a ticket to Birmingham?
Traveller	Well —

BR employee	Birmingham's a terrible place! It's awful! If I were you, I wouldn't go to Birmingham.
Traveller	I live there.
BR employee	Now, Oxford's a very nice place.
Traveller	I *live* there.
BR employee	Why don't you go to Oxford?
Traveller	I *live* there!
BR employee	What? In Oxford?
Traveller	No! In Birmingham!
BR employee	Oh.
Traveller	And I want to go to Birmingham. Today.
BR employee	Impossible.
Traveller	What?
BR employee	It's impossible. It'll take you three days.
Traveller	Three days?
BR employee	Oh, yes. It'll take you at least three days — walking.
Traveller	Walking?! I don't want to *walk* to Birmingham!
BR employee	You don't want to walk?
Traveller	No.
BR employee	Oh, I understand.
Traveller	Good.
BR employee	You want to run.
Traveller	Run?!
BR employee	You'll get very tired if you run.
Traveller	Listen —
BR employee	If I were you, I'd walk.
Traveller	I don't want to walk, and I don't want to run. I want to take the train.
BR employee	The train? Ha! You'll get there much faster if you walk.
Traveller	Now, don't be ridiculous. I want a ticket for the next train to Birmingham.
BR employee	The next train to Birmingham?
Traveller	Yes. When is it?
BR employee	Pardon?
Traveller	What time is it?
BR employee	I don't know. I haven't got a watch.
Traveller	No! I mean: What time is the train? What time does the train leave?
BR employee	Oh, I see. Sorry. I'll check.

II   *He picks up the telephone and dials a number.*

BR employee	Take a seat.
Traveller	Thank you.

The traveller sits down.

BR employee	(*On the phone:*) Hallo? Bert? . . . Who's that? . . . Oh, hallo, Charlie. Where's Bert? . . . Is he? Oh, well, is Eric there? . . . Hallo? Eric? . . . Isn't Bert there? . . . Oh, dear — very sad. Is Arthur there? . . . Hallo? Arthur? . . . Who? Oh, hallo, Charlie. Is Bert there?

The traveller is getting impatient.

Traveller	Look — can you please find out when the next train to Birmingham leaves?
BR employee	Yes, all right. (*On the phone:*) Er . . . Charlie . . . Who's that? Eric? . . . Oh, Arthur. Can I speak to Dave? . . . Yes, OK, I'll hold on.

III

The traveller is getting more impatient.

Traveller	Look —
BR employee	It's all right. I'm holding on. (*On the phone:*) Dave? . . . Hallo, Dave. This is Sid. . . . Very well, thanks — and you? . . . Good. Listen, Dave, there's something I must ask you. How's your wife? . . . Did she?
Traveller	The next train to Birmingham!
BR employee	Oh, yes. (*On the phone:*) Dave, I've got a young man here. When is the next train to Birmingham? Yes . . . Yes . . . Yes . . . Yes . . . Yes. Thanks, Dave. Hold on.
Traveller	Well?
BR employee	He doesn't know.
Traveller	He doesn't know?
BR employee	No.
Traveller	Why not?
BR employee	Well, Dave doesn't work at the station.
Traveller	He doesn't work at the station?!
BR employee	No. Dave works at the café across the road. You should never ask Dave about trains.
Traveller	*I* didn't ask him. *You* asked him!
BR employee	*Eric's* the one who knows about trains.
Traveller	Well, ask *Eric* then.
BR employee	Right. (*On the phone:*) Er . . . Dave, can you put Eric back on? . . . Eric? . . . Eric, I've got a young man here. It's about trains to Birmingham. When is the next one? . . . Right . . . OK . . . Fine . . . Super . . . Smashing . . . Super . . . Fine . . . OK . . . Right. Thanks, Eric. Bye.

He puts down the telephone.

IV

Traveller	So, when is the train?
BR employee	The train, yes. Well, there's a small problem.
Traveller	What's that?
BR employee	They can't find it.
Traveller	They can't find what?
BR employee	They can't find the train. It's lost.
Traveller	Lost?!
BR employee	Well, it's not exactly *lost*. They know where it is.
Traveller	Well, where is it?
BR employee	It's somewhere between here and Birmingham.
Traveller	This is terrible.
BR employee	Yes, but it happens every day. If I were you, I'd start walking.
Traveller	But I'm in a hurry.
BR employee	Well, run then.
Traveller	I don't want to run.
BR employee	Well, take a taxi!
Traveller	I don't want to take a taxi!

The telephone rings. The traveller answers it.

Traveller   Hallo!!! . . . It's for you.

V   *The BR employee takes the telephone.*

BR employee   Thank you. (*On the phone:*) Hallo? Sid speaking. Who's that? . . . Eric! Hallo! What is it? . . . The train to Birmingham? . . . What? . . . Marvellous. Where was it? . . . At Platform 2? . . . It was there all the time. Amazing. . . . OK, Eric, I'll tell him. Bye.

He puts down the telephone.

BR employee   Well, there *is* a train to Birmingham.

Traveller   Marvellous.

BR employee   It's at Platform 2.

Traveller   Wonderful.

BR employee   And it's leaving any minute now.

Traveller   Oh, good. A second-class single to Birmingham, please.

BR employee   Pardon?

Traveller   Can you give me a second-class single to Birmingham?

BR employee   No, I can't.

Traveller   Why not?

BR employee   Well, this isn't the ticket office.

Traveller   What?!

BR employee   The ticket office is next door.

Traveller   Oh, no!

BR employee   What's the matter?

Traveller   I'm going to miss the train!

BR employee   Don't worry. You've got plenty of time.

Traveller   Plenty of time? The train's leaving any minute now.

BR employee   Yes, but there's no hurry.

Traveller   Why not?

BR employee   Because I'm the driver.

Traveller   You're the driver?

BR employee   Yes. The train can't leave without me, can it?

Traveller   No.

BR employee   Now, you come with me.

Traveller   Platform 2?

BR employee   No. Dave's café.

Traveller   Oh, right.

BR employee   We'll have a nice cup of tea and a sandwich before we go.

Traveller   Lovely.

BR employee   And I'll introduce you to Dave and his wife. I think you'll like them . . .

They leave the office, chatting.

About the sketch

Correct these statements.

I
1. The traveller wanted to leave Birmingham as soon as possible.
2. The BR employee said it would take three days by train.
3. The employee did not know the time because his watch was broken.

II
4. He was anxious to find out the time of the train for the traveller.

III
5. Dave works at the station, but he did not know the time of the train.
6. Eric works in a café across the road.

IV
7. The train was lost somewhere in Birmingham.
8. The employee said that British Rail did not usually lose trains.

V
9. The train was at Platform 2 and left a few minutes ago.
10. They had to leave immediately because the BR employee was the driver.

Communicating

1 Buying a ticket and finding out about trains

Look at these lines from the sketch:

I want a ticket for the next train to Birmingham.	Why?
I want to go to Birmingham today.	Impossible.
What time does the train leave?	I don't know.
Can you give me a second-class single to Birmingham?	No, I can't.

The BR employee's replies were not very helpful!
Here are some more helpful replies:

First-class or second-class?
Do you want to reserve a seat?
Smoking or non-smoking?
Do you want to pay by cheque?
....
The train leaves from Platform 4.
There's a train every twenty minutes.

Practise in pairs. One person is a traveller, and one person is a BR employee.

2 Giving advice

Look at these lines from the sketch:

If I were you, I wouldn't go to Birmingham.
You'll get very tired if you run. If I were you, I'd walk.
You should never ask Dave about trains.

Give advice to someone who is going to visit your country. Answer the questions below, using *If I were you, . . .* and *You should . . .* where possible.

Which places should I visit?
Which places should I avoid?
What food should I try?
Can I hitch-hike?
What souvenirs should I buy?
What clothes should I bring with me?

Question time

Here are ten answers. (1–5 are about the sketch; 6–10 are not about the sketch.) What are the questions?

1. . . . .? He was in a hurry.
2. . . . .? He thinks it's a terrible place.
3. . . . .? He asked him about his wife.
4. . . . .? At the café across the road.
5. . . . .? A second-class single to Birmingham.
6. . . . .? No, first-class is more expensive.
7. . . . .? No, it's usually quicker by plane.
8. . . . .? You can reserve a seat.
9. . . . .? A fast train which doesn't stop at all the stations.
10. . . . .? An engine-driver.

Reading: Railway timetables

Look at the time table below, and make a list of things which are wrong or unusual.

LONDON-EDINBURGH	INTER-CITY EXPRESS		
LONDON	DEP:	8.59	
BIRMINGHAM *	DEP:	9.10	* (Change for Coventry: Train departs 9.06)
	ARR:	9.15	
PARIS	ARR:	12.32	
	DEP:	12.36	
MANCHESTER †	ARR:	15.26	† (Change for Birmingham: Train departs 15.45)
	DEP:	3.30pm	
GLASGOW	ARR:	18.64	

Writing: Completing a text

Fill in the missing words, and then finish the story.

Peter Jones wanted to travel to Birmingham. He decided to go by . . . . He went to the . . . station, and waited in a . . . of people to buy a . . . . After five minutes, he reached the window.
'Birmingham; please,' he said.
'That'll be five pounds,' said the ticket-. . . .
Peter took £10 out of his . . . and gave it to the man. He put the ticket in his . . . and walked to . . . 3. The . . . was there. Peter got on, and the . . . began to move. Suddenly, Peter realized something. . . .

In your own words

R-enact the sketch in your own words, without reading from the text. Do it in short sections. These words will remind you.

I	II	III	IV	V
ticket Why? Oxford impossible walk	Bert? leave? speak to Dave?	next train? café Ask Eric	a problem lost start walking a taxi	Platform 2 any minute now next door café

Word puzzle

Fill in the correct answers. Then re-arrange the letters in the vertical box to make a word — something you find at a station. (All the answers are words from the sketch.)

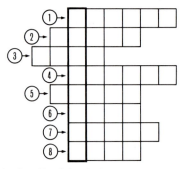

1 A nice English city!
2 The traveller wanted to catch one.
3 Where Dave works.
4 You need one to travel.
5 It tells the time.
6 If you can't find something, it's . . .
7 Birmingham's a terrible . . . !
8 The opposite of 'catch (a train)'.

Extra!

Initials

In the sketch, the 'ticket-seller' is called a *BR employee*. *BR* are the initials of *British Rail*, so we say that BR *stands for* British Rail.

Here are some more well-known initials. What do they stand for?

BBC and *ITV* are two of the television services in Britain.

People sometimes call Britain *GB* or the *UK*. Our national airline is called *BA*. Two other well-known airlines are *TWA* and *QANTAS*. The *RAF* is not an airline, but it is connected with flying.

You see the letters *RR* on the front of our most famous and expensive car.

Finally, what do the letters *ETT* stand for?

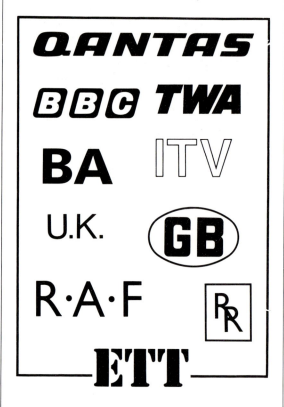

56

8 Gerry Thatcher's party

Scene A smart party

Characters Gerry Thatcher, the host
Maxwell, Gerry's butler
Horace Smith ⎱ guests at
Amanda Spencer ⎰ the party

I *The door-bell rings. Maxwell opens the door.*

Maxwell Yes, sir?

Horace Er . . . Hallo. Is this Gerry Thatcher's house?

Maxwell Yes, sir.

Horace Oh, good. I've got an invitation to Gerry's party. My name's Horace Smith.

Maxwell In that case, please come in, sir.

Horace Thank you.

Maxwell Mr Thatcher is in the lounge. This way.

Horace Er . . . Thank you.

They go into the lounge, where the party is in progress. Horace sees Gerry.

Horace Er . . . Hallo.

Gerry	George!
Horace	What?
Gerry	George Wilberforce!
Horace	Pardon?
Gerry	How are you, George?
Horace	Actually, I'm not —
Gerry	Good, good, good!
Horace	No, just a minute —
Gerry	How's your wife?
Horace	I'm not married.
Gerry	Good, good, good!

The door-bell rings again.

Gerry	Maxwell, give George a drink. I'll go to the door.
Maxwell	Yes, sir.

Gerry opens the door.

Amanda	Gerry!
Gerry	Amanda! How are you?
Amanda	Fine.
Gerry	Good, good, good! Come in, come in, come in.
Amanda	Thank you.

II   *Gerry brings Amanda over to Horace.*

Gerry	Amanda, I'd like you to meet one of my oldest friends — George Wilberforce.
Amanda	How do you do, George.
Horace	Actually, my name *isn't* George.
Gerry	Isn't it?
Horace	No.
Gerry	What is it, then?
Horace	It's Horace Smith, actually.
Gerry	Of course it is! Amanda, I'd like you to meet one of my *dearest* friends, Horace Smith-Actually.
Horace	It's just *Smith,* actually.
Gerry	That's what I said.
Amanda	I'm very pleased to meet you, Mr Actually.
Horace	No, it's *Smith,* actually.
Amanda	Oh, yes. Mr Smith-Actually.
Horace	No, no, no . . . My name isn't Smith-Actually, actually. It's just *Smith,* actually.
Gerry	I'm sure it is. Have a drink. Amanda?
Amanda	Yes, Gerry?
Gerry	Come and have a look at the garden.
Amanda	OK.

Amanda goes into the garden with Gerry.

III

Maxwell	Your drink, sir.
Horace	Thank you. She's very nice, isn't she?
Maxwell	Yes, sir. Very nice indeed.
Horace	I'd like to go out with her.
Maxwell	Would you, sir?
Horace	Yes, very much. The trouble is, I never know what to say when I meet people.
Maxwell	In that case, sir, I think you need this book.

Maxwell shows Horace a book.

Horace	What is it?
Maxwell	'English for all situations', sir. It's full of useful expressions. Look — 'Unit 1: In a restaurant.'. . . 'Unit 2: On a train.' . . . 'Unit 3: At a party. Useful expressions in English, when you meet someone at a party.'
Horace	Wonderful.

Maxwell	(*Reading:*) 'Are you doing anything on Saturday night?'
Horace	No, I'm not, actually.
Maxwell	No, sir. That's the first question. Try it.
Horace	Ah. Are you doing anything on Saturday night?
Maxwell	Good. 'How about going to the cinema?'
Horace	How about going to the cinema?
Maxwell	'What time shall I pick you up?'
Horace	Pardon?
Maxwell	That's the next expression.
Horace	Ah. What time shall I pick you up?
Maxwell	I think, sir, that you should suggest doing something before going to the cinema.
Horace	Good idea. What, for example?

Maxwell		Well, going to a restaurant — an Italian restaurant, perhaps.
Horace		OK.
Maxwell		So you say: 'Do you like Italian food?'
Horace		Do you like Italian food?
Maxwell		*She'll* say 'Yes', because everyone likes Italian food. So *you* say. 'So do I.'
Horace		So do I.
Maxwell		'Let's have *spaghetti alle vongole* before we go.'
Horace		Let's have *spaghetti on a gondola* before we go.
Maxwell		Hmm . . . And finally you say: 'See you on Saturday!'
Horace		See you on Saturday!

IV

Maxwell		Good. Now let's practise.
Horace		Right. Um . . . Are you doing anything on Saturday morning?
Maxwell		Night.
Horace		Oh, good night.
Maxwell		Saturday *night*, sir. Try again.
Horace		Are you doing anything on Saturday night?
Maxwell		(*In a high voice:*) No, I'm not.
Horace		What? . . . Oh, I see. Er . . . good. How about going to the cinema?
Maxwell		(*In a high voice:*) I'd love to.
Horace		What time . . . shall I pick you up?
Maxwell		(*In a high voice:*) Eight o'clock?
Horace		Do you like Italian food?
Maxwell		(*In a high voice:*) Yes, I *love* Italian food.
Horace		So do I. Let's have . . . *spaghetti alle vongole* before we go.
Maxwell		(*In a high voice:*) That would be lovely.
Horace		See you on Saturday!
Maxwell		Very good, sir. Now, take the book, and have a little practice before she comes back.
Horace		Right. Thank you.

V

Horace concentrates on the book. Gerry and Amanda come back from the garden, laughing.

Amanda		Oh, Gerry, you're awfully funny!
Gerry		Yes, I know. Amanda?
Amanda		Yes, Gerry?
Gerry		Are you doing anything on Saturday night?
Amanda		No, I'm not.
Gerry		Super! How about going to the cinema?
Amanda		Oh, Gerry, that would be wonderful.
Gerry		Super! What time shall I pick you up?
Amanda		Eight o'clock?
Gerry		Super!

The door-bell rings again.

Gerry		It's all right, Maxwell — I'll go. See you on Saturday, Amanda!

Amanda	OK, Gerry.

Gerry goes to open the door. Amanda goes over to Horace.

Amanda	Oh, hallo. I don't think we've met.
Horace	Yes, we have, Amanda. It's me, Horace.
Amanda	Horace?
Horace	Yes. Horace Smith.
Amanda	Oh, yes — Mr Actually.

They laugh.

Horace	Er . . . Amanda?
Amanda	Yes, Horace?

Horace looks at the book.

Horace	(*Reading:*) 'Are you doing anything on Saturday night?'
Amanda	Yes, I am.
Horace	(*Still reading:*) 'Good. How about going to the cinema?'
Amanda	Actually, I'm going to the cinema with Gerry on Saturday night.

Horace	'What time shall I pick you up?'
Amanda	Horace, I'm going out with *Gerry* on Saturday night.
Horace	'Do you like Italian food?'
Amanda	No, I *hate* Italian food.
Horace	'So do I. Let's have *spaghetti on a gondola* before we go.'
Amanda	Oh, Horace, you *are* funny. Why don't we go for a walk in the garden?
Horace	'See you on Saturday!'
Amanda	(*Laughing:*) Oh, Horace!

They go into the garden.

About the sketch

Say if these sentences are *true* or *false*.

I   1   Horace's real name is George Wilberforce.

     2   Horace is not married.

II   3   Amanda met Horace for the first time at the party.

     4   Horace is one of Gerry's oldest friends.

III   5   Horace is not very confident when he meets people.

     6   Maxwell has a book which can help Horace.

IV   7   At the party, Horace asked Maxwell to go to the cinema with him.

     8   Horace took the book home to practise.

V   9   Gerry invited Horace and Amanda to go to the cinema.

V   10   Amanda invited Horace to go for a walk in the garden.

Communicating

1   Meeting and greeting people, and introducing people to each other

Look at these lines from the sketch:

> How are you, George?
> How's your wife?
> I'd like you to meet one of my oldest friends.
> I'm very pleased to meet you.
> I don't think we've met.

Here are some more expressions. Decide if they are useful for:
— greeting someone you know,
— meeting someone for the first time,
— introducing two people to each other.

> Lovely to see you again.
> How do you do?
> You must meet George.
> Have you two met before?
> Amanda, this is George.
> It's been such a long time.
> What do you do?

Practise using this language in groups of three.

2   Inviting someone to go out with you

Look at these lines from the sketch:

> Are you doing anything on Saturday night?
> How about going to the cinema?
> What time shall I pick you up?
> Let's have (something to eat) before we go.
> See you on Saturday.

Use those expressions and practise in pairs. One person invites the other:
— to a party
— to a football match
— to the theatre
— to go sailing
— to go for a drive in the country.

Question time

Here are the answers to ten questions about the sketch. What are the questions?

1 ....?   His real name is Horace Smith.
2 ....?   He spoke to the butler, Maxwell.
3 ....?   No, he thought Horace was someone else.
4 ....?   No, he met her for the first time at the party.
5 ....?   He never knows what to say when he meets people.
6 ....?   It's a book full of useful expressions.
7 ....?   He invited Amanda to go to the cinema, and she accepted.
8 ....?   He didn't listen to her replies because he was reading the book.
9 ....?   No, she hates it.
10 ....?   Amanda took Horace for a walk in the garden.

Reading: Invitations

Each of these invitations has a mistake in it.
Find the mistakes.

GERRY THATCHER
invites you to
A PARTY
on February 30th
at his home in Chelsea

You are invited to the
wedding of
DOREEN SMITH and FRED JONES
on July 1st

Church service at 3.00,
followed by lunch at the
Savoy Hotel

This is a complimentary ticket for
the première of the film
THE INCREDIBLE MONSTER
at the Ritz Cinema.
(Please pay £5 at the door.)

Bring your friends to
THE GOLDFISH DISCOTHEQUE
Open 12pm until midnight
seven nights a week

INVITATION

TO AN EXHIBITION OF
PAINTINGS BY
PICASSO, REMBRANDT
AND SHAKESPEARE

AT THE
JOCELYN PLINTH GALLERY

Writing: Completing a text

Complete this telephone conversation.

Jane Hallo, Peter, it's Jane. Are you doing anything on Saturday night?

Peter . . . . . .

Jane Oh, good. How about going to the cinema?

Peter . . . . . .

Jane Why not?

Peter . . . . . .

Jane You can wash your hair on Friday night. I've got two tickets for 'The Incredible Monster'.

Peter . . . . . .

Jane Have you? Did you like it?

Peter . . . . . .

Jane Oh. Well, never mind.

In your own words

Re-enact the sketch in your own words, without reading from the text. Do it in short sections. These words will remind you.

Word puzzle

Below are the 'names' of three of the characters in the sketch. However, there are numbers instead of letters.
First of all, work out what the three names are.
(Look at the length of each word.)

| 8 | 2 | 0 | 10 | 1 | 4 | | 0 | 3 | 6 | 7 | 8 |

| 3 | 10 | 0 | 5 | 4 | 0 | 0 |

| 10 | 3 | 10 | 9 | 0 | 10 |

Have you got all the letters? Now work out the simple thing that Horace wanted to say to Amanda:

1	2	3	4		5	6	7	8		3	4	

	7	2		7	8	4		1	6	9	4	3	10

Extra!

Party expressions

Gerry had a *party* at his house. Here are some expressions using the word *party*. Find out what they mean.
— a political party
— third-party insurance
— a party-line
— a party-wall
— a search party
— the guilty party

9 *The lost property office*

Scene A lost property office

Characters The lost property office clerk
A gangster
A policeman

I   *The gangster runs into the lost property office. There are police cars passing in the street at high speed.*

Clerk Can I help you?
Gangster Where am I?
Clerk You're in a lost property office.
Gangster A lost property office?
Clerk Yes. Have you lost something?
Gangster Probably.
Clerk What have you lost?
Gangster I've lost my . . . umbrella.
Clerk Ah, you want the Umbrella Section.
Gangster The Umbrella Section?

Clerk	Yes. Go out into the street, turn left, and it's on the left.
Gangster	Into the street?
Clerk	Yes. You see, this isn't the Umbrella Section. This is the Animal Section.
Gangster	The Animal Section?
Clerk	Yes.
Gangster	In that case, I've lost my dog.
Clerk	You've lost your dog.
Gangster	Yes.
Clerk	Well, in that case, you want the *Small* Animal Section.
Gangster	The *Small* Animal Section?
Clerk	Yes. Go into the street, turn right, and it's on the right.
Gangster	Into the street?
Clerk	Yes. You see, this isn't the *Small* Animal Section. This is the *Large* Animal Section.
Gangster	The *Large* Animal Section?
Clerk	Yes.
Gangster	In that case, I've lost my elephant.
Clerk	You've lost your elephant?
Gangster	Yes.
Clerk	I see. Well, I'll need a few details. Would you like to sit down?
Gangster	I'd love to.

The gangster sits down.

II

Clerk	Now, first of all: Name.
Gangster	Er . . . Winston.
Clerk	Well, Mr Winston —
Gangster	No, *my* name isn't Winston. The elephant's name is Winston.
Clerk	I see. And what is *your* name?
Gangster	Churchill.
Clerk	(*Writing*:) Churchill. Address?
Gangster	Er . . . Churchill's Circus.
Clerk	Oh, I see. It's a circus elephant.
Gangster	Is it? . . . . Yes. Yes, it is!
Clerk	When did you last see him?
Gangster	Who?
Clerk	The elephant.
Gangster	Oh, Winston. Well, we were on a bus yesterday —
Clerk	On a bus?!
Gangster	Yes.
Clerk	How did Winston get on a bus?
Gangster	How did Winston get on a bus?
Clerk	Yes.
Gangster	That's a very good question. Well . . . He waited at the bus stop, and when the bus came along, he put out his arm. And when the bus stopped, he got on.
Clerk	I see. And then what happened?
Gangster	Well, we were upstairs on the bus —

Clerk	Upstairs?!
Gangster	Yes. Winston wanted to smoke a cigarette.
Clerk	A cigarette?!
Gangster	I know — I tell him every day: 'Winston, smoking is bad for you'. But he never listens.
Clerk	Hmm. What happened then?
Gangster	Well, I fell asleep.
Clerk	You fell asleep?
Gangster	Yes.
Clerk	I see. And then what happened?
Gangster	I don't know — I was asleep. But then I woke up, and Winston wasn't there.

III

Clerk	Hmm. Well, I'd better ask you a few questions about him. What kind of elephant is he?
Gangster	Oh, he's very nice — generous, loving . . . he likes collecting stamps.
Clerk	No — when I say 'What kind of elephant?', I mean: Is he an *African* elephant?
Gangster	Oh, no.
Clerk	So he's an *Indian* elephant.
Gangster	No.
Clerk	What kind of elephant is he?
Gangster	Scottish.
Clerk	A Scottish elephant?!
Gangster	Yes. He wears a kilt.
Clerk	I see. What colour is he?
Gangster	Colour? Well, he's elephant-coloured.
Clerk	And what colour is that?
Gangster	Blue.
Clerk	Blue?!
Gangster	It was very cold yesterday.
Clerk	Yes, it was. Next question: Colour of eyes.

Gangster	Well, you know, like an elephant.
Clerk	What colour is that?
Gangster	Red.
Clerk	Red?!
Gangster	Green.
Clerk	Green?!
Gangster	One red, one green.
Clerk	One red, one green?!
Gangster	Yes. We call him 'Traffic Lights'.
Clerk	I see. Colour of hair?
Gangster	Hair?
Clerk	Yes.
Gangster	He hasn't got any hair.
Clerk	I see. (*Writing:*) Bald. . . . So we're looking for a bald, blue, Scottish elephant, wearing a kilt and smoking a cigarette.
Gangster	Yes.
Clerk	Is there anything unusual about him?
Gangster	No, nothing at all.
Clerk	Good. Now, Mr Churchill, what should we do if we find Winston?
Gangster	Well . . . Put a banana in your hand, walk up to Winston, and say 'Kootchie-kootchie-koo'.
Clerk	What will Winston do?
Gangster	Well, if it's Winston, he'll sit down and he'll eat the banana.
Clerk	All right, Mr Churchill. Just wait a moment, and I'll call the Elephant Section.
Gangster	Fine.

IV

The clerk picks up the telephone and dials a number.

Clerk	Hallo? George? . . . It's Brenda . . . I'm fine, thank you — and you? . . . Good. George, have you got any elephants? . . . You haven't? Hold on a moment. (*To the gangster:*) He hasn't got any elephants.
Gangster	No elephants? Well, not to worry. Sorry to have troubled you. Thank you for your help. I'll be on my way. Goodbye.

He gets up. A police car passes in the street. He sits down again.

Gangster	Er . . . Ask George to have another look.
Clerk	All right. (*On the phone:*) George, can you have another look?
Gangster	Tell him to look under the table.
Clerk	Look under the table. . . . What? . . . (*To the gangster:*) He's got one.
Gangster	A table?
Clerk	No, an *elephant*.
Gangster	An *elephant*?
Clerk	Yes. It was under the table.
Gangster	Really?
Clerk	(*On the phone:*) Yes, George, I'm listening . . . Yes . . . Yes . . . Yes . . . Yes. Hold on. (*To the gangster:*) He's got a bald, blue, Scottish elephant, wearing a kilt and smoking a cigarette. It sounds like Winston.

Gangster	What about the banana?
Clerk	Oh, yes. (*On the phone:*) George . . . I want you to put a banana in your hand, and say 'Kootchie-kootchie-koo'. . . . . No, not to *me* — to the *elephant*. OK? . . . What? . . . Oh, no!
Gangster	What's the matter?
Clerk	The elephant sat down.
Gangster	Good.
Clerk	On George.
Gangster	Tell George to give Winston the banana!
Clerk	Right. (*On the phone:*) George? George! . . . Get up and give the banana to the elephant. . . . Hallo? . . . What? . . . Oh, no!
Gangster	What is it?
Clerk	He's eaten the banana.
Gangster	Who? Winston?
Clerk	No. George.
Gangster	Oh, no!
Clerk	(*On the phone:*) George, I think you should bring the elephant down here. The owner is waiting to take him away. . . . OK . . . Bye.

The clerk puts down the telephone.

V

Clerk	Don't worry, Mr Churchill. Your elephant will be here in a moment.
Gangster	Look — before this elephant arrives, there's something you should know —

They hear the sound of an elephant.

Clerk	Ah, that must be Winston.

They hear the sound of someone falling over.

Clerk	And that's George.

Someone knocks at the door.

Clerk	Go on, Mr Churchill. Open the door.
Gangster	Oh, all right.

He opens the door.

Gangster	Hallo, Winston. Kootchie-kootchie-koo!
Policeman	Mr Churchill?
Gangster	But . . . this isn't an elephant. It's a policeman.
Policeman	Very good, sir. Now, if you'd like to follow me . . .
Clerk	Goodbye, Mr Churchill. And don't forget: If you lose your elephant again, the Lost Property Office is here to help you.
Gangster	Oh, good. I'll remember that.

He leaves with the policeman.

About the sketch

Say if these sentences are *true* or *false*, according to the sketch.

I   1   The gangster said he lost an umbrella, a dog and an elephant.

      2   The Umbrella Section is across the street.

II   3   The elephant's name is Winston Churchill.

      4   The gangster last saw his elephant on a bus.

III   5   Winston is a Scottish elephant with green eyes.

      6   There is nothing unusual about the elephant.

IV   7   The gangster wanted George to have another look because it was cold in the street.

      8   George found an elephant on his table.

V   9   The gangster decided to tell the truth about his situation.

    10   Winston is, in fact, a policeman.

Communicating

1   Describing people and things

Look at these lines from the sketch:

What kind of elephant is he?	He's very nice . . .
What colour is he?	Elephant-coloured.
Colour of eyes?	One red, one green.
Is there anything unusual about him?	No, nothing at all.

Note: When the characters in the sketch talk about the elephant, they use *he/him* instead of *it*. This is because they know the elephant is male, and they talk about him as if he were human. A lot of people talk about their pet animals in this way (*he/him/his* or *she/her/her* instead of *it/its*).

You will probably not have to describe an elephant very often, but you can use this language to describe

— one of your pets   — a member of your family
— one of your friends   — your teacher.
Here are some more useful questions and answers:

How $\begin{Bmatrix} old \\ tall \\ big \end{Bmatrix}$ is $\begin{Bmatrix} she \\ he \end{Bmatrix}$?

What does $\begin{Bmatrix} he \\ she \end{Bmatrix}$ look like?

What is $\begin{Bmatrix} he \\ she \end{Bmatrix}$ like?

She's/He's tall/short/fair/dark/slim/kind/intelligent . . .

2   Describing a series of events

Read Section **II** of the sketch again. The gangster described a series of events. Describe a series of events which happened to you, and let the other students ask you questions as you do it.

Yesterday, I was . . . Then I went . . .
Suddenly, I saw . . .
Eventually, I decided to . . .
Finally, I went . . .

What happened? What happened next? Then what happened?
Really? Are you sure? You're kidding!
That's amazing!

Question time

Here are the answers to ten questions about the sketch. What are the questions?

    1   . . . . ?   Because the police were after him.

    2   . . . . ?   Because he did not want to go back into the street.

    3   . . . . ?   No, he knew very little about elephants.

    4   . . . . ?   No, all elephants are either African or Indian.

    5   . . . . ?   A kind of skirt worn by Scotsmen.

    6   . . . . ?   Traffic lights.

    7   . . . . ?   The man who works in the Elephant Section.

    8   . . . . ?   It means 'having no hair'.

    9   . . . . ?   A policeman.

  10   . . . . ?   He took the gangster to the police station.

Reading: Who is speaking?

Read these statements. They are by characters from the sketch, talking about events in the sketch. Say who is speaking each time.

1 'I was in my office when the telephone rang. It was Brenda.'
2 'A man opened the door and said "Kootchie-kootchie-koo" to me.'
3 'I ran through a door. I didn't know where I was.'
4 'A man came into my office. I asked him if I could help him.'
5 'I told the man to follow me.'
6 'She told me to put a banana in my hand.'
7 'I wrote down the man's name and address.'
8 'She asked me to describe the elephant.'

Writing:
A narrative and a form

1 Write an account of what happened when you lost something.

2 Fill in the form below with details of the elephant in the sketch. Then fill it in with details of one of your pets (if you have any), or with invented details of another animal.

```
                LOST ANIMAL
OWNER'S NAME: ............................................
OWNER'S ADDRESS: ......................................
TYPE OF ANIMAL: ..........................................
ORIGIN: .........................................................
COLOUR: ......................................................
COLOUR OF EYES: ........................................
PREFERRED FOOD: ........................................
ANSWERS TO THE NAME OF: ............................
WHERE LOST: ................................................
```

In your own words

Re-enact the sketch in your own words, without reading from the text. Do it in short sections. These words will remind you.

I	II	III	IV	V
Can I help you? umbrella dog elephant	Winston/ Churchill circus bus upstairs	What kind? What colour? eyes hair banana	George under the table banana	in a moment policeman Follow me

Word puzzle

Fill in the correct answers in the horizontal boxes. (All the words appeared in the sketch.) You will then find a word in the vertical box — a good word to describe Mr Churchill's story.

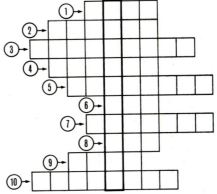

1 A Scotsman sometimes wears one.
2 A girl's name.
3 Britain's Prime Minister in the 1940s.
4 A man's name.
5 A large animal.
6 A small animal.
7 3's first name.
8 A means of public transport.
9 Having no hair.
10 It keeps you dry in the rain.

Extra!

The Lost Property Top 10

The sketch was about a Lost Property Office. People often lose things on public transport, and all public transport services have Lost Property Offices. The things below are the 'Top 10' most commonly lost things on British Rail (Southern Region) trains. The list is not in the correct order, however. What do you think is the correct order? (The answer is at the bottom of the page.)

Coats	Suitcases and trunks
Jewellery	Wallets and purses
Gloves	Umbrellas
Spectacles	Sports bags
Briefcases	Plastic shopping bags, with contents

This is the correct order for the 'Top 10': 1. Umbrellas (12 200 per year); 2. Plastic shopping bags, with contents (7000); 3. Coats (5500); 4. Wallets and purses (3500); 5. Gloves (3300); 6. Sports bags (2200); 7. Spectacles (1900) & Suitcases and trunks (also 1900); 9. Jewellery (1300); 10. Briefcases (1200).

10 Mr Universe

Scene The 'Mr Universe' competition

Characters Gloria Sparkle, the presenter
Arnold Higgins ⎫
Elvis Smith ⎬ the contestants
Ernest Bottom ⎭

I   ***The competition is just beginning.***

Gloria Yes, ladies and gentlemen, it's time once again for the 'Mr Universe' competition — the competition to find the most *fantastic*, the most *incredible*, the most *amazing* man in the world.
Who will be this year's Mr Universe? Our three judges will decide. But first let's meet the contestants. Contestant Number 1 — Arnold Higgins!

Arnold Higgins enters, carrying a bucket and a sponge.

II   Gloria Ladies and gentlemen, this is Arnold Higgins.
Arnold Hallo!
Gloria (*Reading from a card in her hand:*) Arnold is 63 years old.
Arnold What? No, no, no. 36, not 63.
Gloria Sorry, Arnold.

Arnold	That's all right.
Gloria	Arnold is 36 years old. Tell me, Arnold — what do you do?
Arnold	I'm a window-cleaner.
Gloria	He's a window-cleaner, ladies and gentlemen! And tell me, Arnold — how long have you been a window-cleaner?
Arnold	Well, Gloria, I'm 36 now, and I started cleaning windows when I was 33. So I've been cleaning windows for . . . er . . .
Gloria	Three years?
Arnold	Yes. How did you know?
Gloria	It's written on this card. Do you like it?

Arnold looks at the card.

Arnold	Yes. It's a very nice card.
Gloria	No, no — not the card. Do you like cleaning windows?
Arnold	Do I like cleaning windows?
Gloria	Yes.
Arnold	Do *I like* cleaning windows?
Gloria	Yes.
Arnold	Do *I like cleaning windows*?
Gloria	Yes.
Arnold	No! I don't *like* cleaning windows — I *love* it!
Gloria	You love it.
Arnold	Yes, I love it. Big windows, small windows, broken windows —
Gloria	Yes, I see.
Arnold	Windows are my life! I've cleaned windows all over the world.
Gloria	Really?
Arnold	Yes. Do you know Buckingham Palace?
Gloria	Yes.
Arnold	Do you know the *windows* of Buckingham Palace?
Gloria	Yes. Arnold, have *you* cleaned the windows of Buckingham Palace?
Arnold	No — but I'd like to.
Gloria	Ah, so your *ambition* is to clean the windows of Buckingham Palace.
Arnold	Yes.
Gloria	Thank you, Arnold.

She wants Arnold to go.

Arnold	Before I go, I'd like to tell you about my hobby.
Gloria	What's that, Arnold?
Arnold	My hobby is writing poetry. I'd like to read one of my poems.
Gloria	Oh.
Arnold	It's about windows.
Gloria	Ah.
Arnold	(*Reading:*) 'Oh, windows! Oh, windows! Oh, windows!'
Gloria	Oh, no!

Arnold	'Windows, windows, big and small! Windows, windows, I love you all!'	
Gloria	Thank you, Arnold.	
Arnold	There's a bit more.	
Gloria	No, thank you, Arnold — that's quite enough. Ladies and gentlemen, the first contestant: Arnold Higgins!	

Arnold leaves.

III

Gloria	Now let's meet the second contestant, who also wants to be this year's Mr Universe!

Elvis Smith enters. He is wearing short trousers and is rather shy.

Elvis	Er . . . Hallo.
Gloria	What is your name?
Elvis	Elvis.
Gloria	Elvis?
Elvis	Yes. Elvis Smith.
Gloria	How old are you, Elvis?
Elvis	42.
Gloria	And what do you do?
Elvis	Nothing. I'm still at school.
Gloria	Still at school?
Elvis	Yes.
Gloria	What do you want to do when you leave school?
Elvis	Go to university.
Gloria	I see. And what is your hobby, Elvis?
Elvis	My hobby?
Gloria	Yes. What do you like doing in your free time?
Elvis	Oh well, I like meeting people. Hallo, Gloria.
Gloria	Hallo, Elvis.
Elvis	And I like fishing.
Gloria	Yes?
Elvis	And swimming.
Gloria	Thank you, Elvis.
Elvis	And collecting stamps, and playing football, and dancing —
Gloria	Thank you, Elvis.
Elvis	And climbing mountains, and water-skiing, and boxing —
Gloria	*Thank you, Elvis!* Ladies and gentlemen, Elvis Smith!

Elvis leaves.

IV

Gloria	Well, ladies and gentlemen, that was Elvis Smith. Now let's meet the last contestant. From Liverpool: Ernest Bottom!

Ernest Bottom enters. He is not very friendly.

Gloria	Well, Ernest, it's wonderful to have you here —
Ernest	All right, get on with it!

Gloria Oh. Well . . . Ernest, would you like to answer a few questions?
Ernest No.
Gloria Oh, come on, Ernest!
Ernest All right — just a few.
Gloria Thank you. Tell me — what do you do?

Ernest What do I do?
Gloria Yes.
Ernest Nothing. I'm unemployed.
Gloria Oh.
Ernest I used to be a bus-driver.
Gloria Did you?
Ernest Yes. But I lost my job.
Gloria Why?
Ernest I can't drive.
Gloria Oh, I see. What do you like doing in your free time?
Ernest Nothing.
Gloria Oh, come on, Ernest! Haven't you got any hobbies?
Ernest Well . . . I've got one. I like gardening. Shall I tell you about my garden?
Gloria Yes!

Ernest   Well . . . it's . . .

Gloria   Yes?

Ernest   It's . . .

Gloria   Yes?

Ernest   It's green!

Gloria sighs.

Gloria   Well, thank you, Ernest. That was fascinating. Ladies and gentlemen, Ernest Bottom.

Ernest leaves.

V   **Gloria**   Well, now we've met the three contestants, and our judges are ready with their votes. For Arnold Higgins: *one* vote. For Elvis Smith: *one* vote. And for Ernest Bottom: *one* vote.
Well, this is sensational, ladies and gentlemen! This year, we have *three* Mr Universes! So, congratulations to our three contestants, and thank you to our judges: Mrs Doris Higgins, Mrs Brenda Smith and Mrs Margaret Bottom. From all of us here, good night!

About the sketch

Choose the correct words.

I 1 The 'Mr Universe' competition takes place once a *week/month/year*.

II 2 Arnold Higgins is *36/63* years old.
   3 He *has/has not* cleaned the windows of Buckingham Palace.
   4 His hobby is *gardening/collecting stamps/writing poetry*.

III 5 Elvis Smith is *older/younger* than Arnold Higgins.
   6 His ambition is to go to *school/ university*.

IV 7 Ernest Bottom *is/was* a bus-driver.
   8 He *has/has not* got a job.
   9 He has *no free time/no hobbies/one hobby*.

V 10 Each contestant received *one vote/two votes/three votes*.

Communicating

1 Talking about interests and hobbies

Look at these lines from the sketch:

Arnold	My hobby is writing poetry.
Gloria	What is your hobby, Elvis?
Elvis	I like meeting people.
Gloria	What do you like doing in your free time?
Ernest	I like gardening.

In Section **III**, Elvis listed his hobbies. Apart from 'meeting people', he listed eight hobbies. What were they?

Ask and answer in pairs:

(Have you got any hobbies? { What do you like doing in your (free time?	I like . . .

Now ask and answer in pairs, about Elvis's hobbies:

Do you like . . . ?	Yes, very much. Not much. No, I don't.

2 Talking about jobs

Look at these lines from the sketch:

> What do you do?
> I'm a window-cleaner.
> How long have you been a window-cleaner?
> Three years.

> What do you do?
> Nothing. I'm unemployed.
> Oh.
> I used to be a bus-driver.

> What do you do?
> I'm still at school.
> What do you want to do when you leave school?
> Go to university.

A Make dialogues in pairs.
A asks *What do you do?* **B** replies, like Arnold, Elvis or Ernest.

B Play 'Guess the job'.
One student thinks of a job. The other students try to find out what the job is, by asking questions:
— Do you work indoors? Outdoors?
— Do you work in a shop? In an office? etc.
Alternatively, students take it in turns to *mime* a job, and the other students guess what the job is.

3 Talking about ambitions

Look at these lines from the sketch:

> Arnold, have *you* cleaned the windows of Buckingham Palace?
> No, but I'd like to.
> Ah, so your *ambition* is to clean the windows of Buckingham Palace.
> Yes.

Find out your friends' ambitions. Ask and answer.

What is your ambition?	(My ambition is) to . . .
Why?	Because . . .

Question time

Here are the answers to ten questions about the sketch. What are the questions.

1 ....? The presenter of the 'Mr Universe' competition.
2 ....? Arnold Higgins, Elvis Smith and Ernest Bottom.
3 ....? 36.
4 ....? 42.
5 ....? He's a window-cleaner.
6 ....? He's still at school.
7 ....? Nothing. He's unemployed.
8 ....? Writing poetry.
9 ....? Gardening.
10 ....? To clean the windows of Buckingham Palace.

Reading:
Correcting mistakes

Read Gloria Sparkle's cards about the 'Mr Universe' contestants, and find the mistakes. There are five *spelling mistakes* and five *mistakes about facts.*

CONTESTANT No. 1	
NAME:	Arnold Higgins
AGE:	63
JOB:	Window-cleaner (for 13 years)
HOBBY:	Writting poetry

CONTESTANT No. 2	
NAME:	Elvis Smith
AGE:	24
JOB:	University student
HOBBIES:	Fishing, swiming, collecting stamps, dancing, water-skiing, boxing, playing football, climbbing mountains and meeting people .

CONTESTANT No. 3	
NAME:	Ernest Bottom
AGE:	?
JOB:	Unemployed. (Used to be a taxi-driver)
HOBBY	Gardenning

Writing: A letter to a pen-friend

This is Elvis Smith's first letter to his pen-friend in France.

15, Charles Street,
London SW 27
May 3rd 1985

Dear Michel,
I'd like to tell you about myself. I'm English and I'm 42 years old. At the moment, I'm still at school. When I leave school, I want to go to university. My ambition is to win the 'Mr. Universe' competition.
In my free time, I like fishing, swimming and meeting people. I've got a lot of other hobbies too.
Please write to me and tell me about yourself.
Best wishes,
Elvis

Monsieur M. Laroche
74 Avenue Martigny
Paris 75010
France

Write a similar letter about yourself. Mention your nationality, age, school/job, hobbies and interests, and ambitions.

In your own words

Re-enact the sketch in your own words, without reading from the text. Do it in short sections. These words will remind you.

I	II	III	IV	V
'Mr Universe' judges contestants	63/36 window-cleaner Buck. Pal. poetry	42 school hobby?	unemployed hobbies? gardening	votes 3 judges Good night!

Word puzzle

Put the correct words in the vertical columns. Then fill in the missing letters to make three hobbies in the horizontal boxes.

1 Arnold read a poem about...
2 One of Ernest's hobbies is climbing...
3 Arnold has... windows all over the world.
4 Arnold's... is to clean the windows of Buckingham Palace.
5 Mr Universe should be the most... man in the world.
6 Arnold's hobby is... poetry.

Extra!

Stamps

One of Elvis Smith's hobbies was collecting stamps. Here are a few stamps from his collection. Which countries are they from?

Here are four more. Which countries are they from? These are a little more difficult.

And here are four stamps from the UK. Do you notice something unusual about UK stamps?

UK stamps do not have the name of the country on them.

79

Language Summary

Sketch	Tenses occurring in sketch	Language areas practised in *Communicating* section
1 Tea break	Present Simple	Asking and explaining how to do something Saying what you'd like to drink Changing your mind
2 The King of Boonland	Present Simple Present Continuous	Telling someone about your country Finding out about someone's country Correcting someone politely
3 The restaurant	Present Simple Present Continuous	Choosing a restaurant Ordering in a restaurant Asking for explanations
4 The passport office	Present Simple Present Continuous was, had	Asking for a giving personal information (informal) Asking for and giving personal information (formal)
5 Fire practice	Present Simple Present Continuous Past Simple	Giving practical hints Talking on the telephone Giving directions
6 The bus stop	Present Simple Present Continuous Past Simple Future Simple going to + Infinitive	Finding out about bus services Talking about language ability Clearing up misunderstandings
7 A ticket to Birmingham	Present S. & C. (inc. for 'future arrangements') Past Simple (inc. '2nd conditional') Future Simple going to + Infinitive	Buying a ticket Finding out about trains Giving advice
8 Gerry Thatcher's party	Present S. & C. (inc. for 'future arrangements') Past Simple Future Simple Present Perfect	Meeting and greeting people Introducing people to each other Inviting someone to go out with you
9 The lost property office	Present Simple Present Continuous Past Simple Future Simple Present Perfect	Describing people and things Describing a series of events
10 Mr Universe	Present Simple Present Continuous Past Simple Future Simple Present Perfect Pres. Perf. Cont. used to + Infinitive	Talking about interests and hobbies Talking about jobs Talking about ambitions